Application of Soft Systems Meth

Model

Dawit Mekonnen

Application of Soft Systems Methodology to develop IS Security Model

LAP LAMBERT Academic Publishing

Imprint

Any brand names and product names mentioned in this book are subject to trademark, brand or patent protection and are trademarks or registered trademarks of their respective holders. The use of brand names, product names, common names, trade names, product descriptions etc. even without a particular marking in this work is in no way to be construed to mean that such names may be regarded as unrestricted in respect of trademark and brand protection legislation and could thus be used by anyone.

Cover image: www.ingimage.com

Publisher:
LAP LAMBERT Academic Publishing
is a trademark of
International Book Market Service Ltd., member of OmniScriptum Publishing Group
17 Meldrum Street, Beau Bassin 71504, Mauritius

Printed at: see last page
ISBN: 978-3-659-89821-1

Zugl. / Approved by: Addis Ababa, Ethiopia, HiLCoE School of Computer Science and Technology, 2017

Copyright © Dawit Mekonnen
Copyright © 2019 International Book Market Service Ltd., member of OmniScriptum Publishing Group

ACKNOWLEDGEMENT

Next to GOD I would like to express my truthful thankfulness to my advisor Dr. Tibebe Beshah for the continuous support for my MSc study and research. His guidance helped me in all the time of research and writing of this thesis. The thesis would not have this shape without his profession inputs, criticism, guidance and support.

I would like to use this opportunity to thank the surveyed banks of Ethiopia such as for branch staffs, IT directors and managers, and specifically IT security Managers who took their time and respond my questionnaire, interview and discussion. I would like to say thank you all for your unreserved cooperation.

Last but not least, I would like to extend my thanks to all my families and friends for their support, encouragement and prayer not only during my thesis work but also all the way during my study.

ABSTRACT

Information has become the most valuable asset to protect from insiders, outsiders and competitors. Information systems security protects all information assets from misuse, harm or any other unintended results by securing information, maintaining integrity of the business process, retaining skilled knowledge workers with their implicit knowledge and also encouraging employees to entitlement ownership of their share of information assets. Organization continue to witness information-related crime and damage becoming the choice of a growing global criminal element. Banking business competition has motivated the advancement of services enabled by IT which in turn increased the IS security risk. In today's banking industry having a good reputation for safeguarding information will increase market share and profit. Nowadays, banks are implementing different types of practices to protect the information and information systems from fraud attacks and other unintended actions.

This research has been conducted in order to identify and explore the issues involved in Information Systems security practices and activities of banking industries in Ethiopia. This research specifies that focusing on the technical aspects of IS security without due consideration of how human interacts with the system is clearly insufficient in safeguarding Ethiopian banks information assets. This research also indicates that maintaining information security requires support and co-operation from all employees within the banks of Ethiopia and the impact of IS security on the banking industries of Ethiopia in safeguarding their information assets is highly complex. Therefore, this research adopts a broader perspective and presents an understanding of IS security in terms of a social and organizational perspective by using the Checkland's Soft Systems Methodology as an approach in order to achieve a greater insight of the problem situation and with the aim of identifying changes which could improve it. Soft Systems Methodology (SSM) is applied to this research. This research has been conducted using mixed research method as a research paradigm and survey questionnaire & interview are used as a method of data collection. The main aim of this research is to develop Information Systems Security model for Ethiopian banking industry using Soft Systems approach by perceiving dynamic behavior of the human aspect and holistic view of information security practices in the Ethiopian banking industry. A survey was conducted with five surveyed banks of Ethiopia and the collected data was used to construct a conceptual model.

This research has been proposed a conceptual model. The conceptual model was compared with the real world in stage five of SSM in table form by five relevant stakeholders and a list of recommendation is presented based on the comparison result obtained from "seven stages" of SSM about the situation. The solutions derived then form the basis upon which recommendations for this research are presented that is both systemically desirable and culturally feasible.

IT security Managers report of their evaluation result of the model, they found the model satisfactory, desirable and culturally feasible in the context of Ethiopia banking industries.

Keywords: Soft Systems Methodology, Information Systems, Information Systems Security

Table of Contents

ACKNOWLEDGEMENT iii
ABSTRACT iv
LIST OF TABLEs I
LIST OF FIGURES II
LIST OF ACRONYMS III
CHAPTER ONE 1
INTRODUCTION 1
   1.1 Background 1
   1.2 Research Motivation 2
   1.3 Statement of the problem 2
   1.4 Research Questions 5
   1.5 Objectives 5
      1.5.1 General Objective 5
      1.5.2 Specific Objectives 5
   1.6 Scope and Limitation 6
   1.7 Application of Result 6
   1.8 Ethical Consideration 6
   1.9 Organization of the Thesis 7
CHATPTER TWO 8
LITERATURE REVIEW AND RELATED WORKS 8
   2.1 Overview 8
   2.2 Soft Systems Methodology (SSM) 8
      2.2.1 Introduction 8
      2.2.2 Seven stages of Soft Systems Methodology 10
   2.3. Information Systems Security 14
   2.4. Commonly used IS security frameworks 15
   2.5. Brief history of Ethiopian banking industry 16
   2.6 Related Works 17
   2.7 Summary 23

CHAPTER THREE 24
METHODOLOGY 24
   3.1 Overview 24
   3.2 Research Design 24
   3.3 Sampling technique and sampling design 24
      3.3.1 Source of data 24
      3.3.2 Population 24
      3.3.3 Sampling method 25
      3.3.4 Sample scope 26
      3.3.5 Sample size 26
   3.4 Data Collection Technique 27
      3.4.1 Questionnaires 27
      3.4.2 Interview 28
   3.5 Pilot Study 28
   3.6 Procedures 29
   3.7 Data Analysis Technique 29
   3.8 Design Technique 30
   3.9 Evaluation Technique 30
   3.10 Summary 31
CHAPTER FOUR 32
FINDINGS INTERPRETATON AND INFERENCES 32
   4.1 Overview 32
   4.2 Respondent Information 32
   4.3 Data collection procedure using questionnaire 32
   4.4 Response rate 33
   4.5 Findings 33
      4.5.1 Questionnaire findings 33
      4.5.2 Interview findings 49
   4.6 Summary 55

CHAPTER FIVE	57
DESIGN OF THE FRAMEWORK USING SSM	57
5.1 Overview	57
5.2 Why do we adopt SSM	57
5.3 Rich picture and summary of the survey	57
5.3.1 Summary of the survey (questionnaire and interview findings)	57
5.3.2 Rich picture	59
5.4 Root Definition of relevant system and Conceptual model	61
5.5 Evaluation (comparison of the model with the rich picture)	70
5.6 Discussion	78
5.7 Summary	79
CHAPTER SIX	80
CONCLUSION AND RECOMMENDATION	80
6.1 Conclusion	80
6.2 Solutions and Recommendations	81
References	84
APPENDIX A	88
APPENDIX B	93
APPENDIX C	93
APPENDIX D	93
APPENDIX E	95
DECLARATION	99

LIST OF TABLES

Table 2.1 Summary of related works 21

Table 2.2 summary of the population of surveyed banks 25

Table 4.1 summary of job status 34

Table 4.2 summary of length of service in the bank 34

Table 4.3 summary of educational background 34

Table 4.4 summary result of the six information security culture dimensions 36

Table 4.2 Summary of questionnaire findings and their recommendations for information systems (IS) security culture statements 46

Table 5.1 List of inter dependent activities for modeling Information systems security system 68

Table 5.2 comparison of the conceptual model with the expressed problem situation 71

LIST OF FIGURES

Figure 2.1 SSM as a Learning cycle (Checkland and Scholes, 1990) 9

Figure 2.2 seven stages of Checkland's methodology (SSM) 10

Figure 2.3 a logical procedure for building activity model 12

Figure 3.1 the general layout for developing the model (IS security Model) 30

Figure 4.1 summary of knowledge level statement questions response 35

Figure 4.2 summary findings of leadership and governance dimension 37

Figure 4.3 summary findings of security management and organization dimension 38

Figure 4.4 summary findings of security program management dimension 39

Figure 4.5 summary finings of user security management dimension 41

Figure 4.6 summary findings of technology protection and operation dimension 42

Figure 4.7 summary findings of change dimension 43

Figure 5.1 rich picture of the IS security activities and processes of Ethiopian banking industry 60

Figure 5.2 conceptual model of Information Systems Security Model 69

LIST OF ACRONYMS

CATWOE	Customers, Actors, Transformation, Weltanschauung, Owner, Environment
COBIT	Control Objectives for Information and related Technologies
FFIEC	Federal Financial Institutions Examination Council
IS	Information System
ISM	Information Security Management
ISMS	Information Security Management System
ISO	International Organization for Standardization
IT	Information Technology
NBE	National Bank of Ethiopia
PCI DSS	Payment Card Industry Data Security Standards
SSM	Soft Systems Methodology

CHAPTER ONE
INTRODUCTION

1.1 Background

Information has become the most valuable asset that should be protected from insiders, outsiders and competitors. As defined by Lee [1] "an information system is not the information technology alone, but the system that emerges from the mutually transformational interaction between the information technology and the organization". The main purpose of IS security is to protect information and specifically to assure the confidentiality, integrity and availability of an organization's data or information assets. Information systems security protects all information assets from misuse, harm or any other unintended results by securing information, maintaining integrity of the business process, retaining skilled knowledge workers with their implicit knowledge and also encouraging employees to entitlement ownership of their share of information assets [2]. Business partners, suppliers, and vendors are seeing security as the top requirement, particularly when providing mutual network and information access.

Organizations continue to witness information-related crime and damage becoming the choice of a growing global criminal element. Existing institutions burdened by countless conflicting jurisdictions and inadequate resources have not been successful in reducing the amount or impact of these activities. Therefore in order to minimize and proactively protect information related crimes and information security breaches, IS security governance must be implemented in the organizations. As Baskerville [3] also noted that the real benefit in IS security is to ensure a "communication link between the security and management professionals". Therefore, a large portion of the task of protecting critical information resources falls squarely on the shoulders of executives and boards of directors. Another work in [4] points that to achieve effectiveness and sustainability in today's complex and interconnected world, IS security must be addressed at the highest levels of the organization not regarded as a technical specialty relegated to the IT/IS department.

Maintaining information security requires support and co-operation from all employees within the organization. Even though technical aspect of IS security needs due attention, a more serious and under-rated aspect of IS security is the human element. Reference [5] underline that the behavior of employees and their interaction with computer systems have a significant impact on the security of information. Many losses are not caused by lack of technology or defective technology rather by users of technology and flawed human behavior. In March 2002, a "logic bomb"' deleted 10 billion files in the computer systems of an international financial services company. The incident affected over 1300 of the company's server throughout the United States. The company sustained losses of approximately $3 million, the amount required to repair damage and reconstruct deleted files. Investigations by law enforcement professionals and computer forensic professionals revealed the logic bomb had been planted by a disgruntled employee who had recently quit the company because of a dis-pate over the amount of his annual bonus.

Banks' ability to take advantage of new opportunities often depends on its ability to provide open, accessible, available, and secure network services. Having a good reputation for safeguarding information will increase market share and profit. Nowadays, banks are implementing different types of practices to protect the information and information systems from fraud attacks. A recent BIS paper indicates that the UK financial sector is already spending over £700 million annually [6]. The issue is also being managed at board level, with 86 % of banking and capital market CEOs identifying technological advances as the trend that will have greatest impact on their businesses [7].

The banking industry in Ethiopia is one of the rapidly growing industry of the country's economy. Author [8] argue that information system has become the heart of modern banking in our world today. Banking business competition has motivated the advancement of services enabled by IT which in turn increased the IS security risk. Banks in Ethiopia must implement a comprehensive IS security model or baseline in order to mitigate IS security risks and to proactively protect any information security related problems.

1.2 Research Motivation

Banking business competition has motivated the advancement of services enabled by IT which in turn increased the IS security risk. Any mishandling or misuse of confidential information asset, security breaches and frauds can scarcely cause financial loss, loss of customers and can have negative impact on the reputation of the banking industry. As financial institutions like banking industry are more sensitive to security issues, priority is given to assess the level of IS security practices. In addition to the above motivation as a senior IT auditor working on banking industry, I was curious on the practices of Information Systems security issues and problems that comes from faulty human factors. When I got the chance to conduct a research I was really happy to inquiry IS security framework for banking industry in Ethiopia.

1.3 Statement of the problem

Information systems security begins and ends with the people within the organization and with the people that interact with the system intentionally or otherwise. The end-users who try to access the information which the security professionals are trying to protect could be the weakest link in security chain. Therefore maintaining information security requires support and co-operation from all employees within the organization. Even though technical aspect of IS security needs due attention, a more serious and under-rated aspect of IS security is the human element. Reference [3] underline that the behavior of employees and their interaction with computer systems have a significant impact on the security of information. Humans are consistently referred to as the weakest link in security [13, 14]. Focus on the technical aspects of security without due consideration of how the human interacts with the system is clearly insufficient.

The importance of non-technical issues related to information security hasn't been given attention in many studies [15]. Consequently little attention has been given to the role of human factor like individual choice and behavior or to organizational factors such as national and organizational culture, environment, information security awareness level of employees and how the factors relate to attitudes of employees about information security. However, empirical studies [15, 16, and 12] have revealed that non-technical issues are very important in safeguarding an organizational sensitive information.

In order to minimize and proactively protect information related crimes and information security breaches an effective IS security control must be implemented in the organizations. As Baskerville [3] also noted that the real benefit in IS security is to ensure a "communication link between the security and management professionals". Therefore, a large portion of the task of protecting critical information resources falls squarely on the shoulders of executives and boards of directors. Another work in [4] points that to achieve effectiveness and sustainability in today's complex and interconnected world, IS security must be addressed at the highest levels of the organization not regarded as a technical specialty relegated to the IT/IS department.

Banking industries in Ethiopia is one of the rapidly growing sectors of the country's economy. In addition, the banking service has shifted from local branch banks to national and global existence and anywhere-anytime banking. The Banking business competition has motivated the advancement of services enabled by IT which in turn increased the information security risk. These threats to information and information systems can include purposeful attacks, environmental disruptions, and human/machine errors and result in great harm to the national and economic security interests of the country [62].

Ethiopian banking system is still underdeveloped compared to the rest of the world regarding electronic payment, Internet banking, and Mobile banking, online shopping etc. such systems are at early or newborn stage. The reason for this weak or evolutionary development is being numerous, the main one that is cited by different scholars is security threat or poor implementation of Information systems security in the country [8][60][61]. Currently, for banking industry there is no information security standards provided and there is no clear guidance regarding what would establish an acceptable minimum baseline body of information security knowledge for end users in the country [60].

The preliminary literature survey and the researcher's experience shows organizations in Ethiopia are at different level of understanding and acting with regard to security activities and various threat mitigations. The author of this research conduct a preliminary assessment on information systems security activities and issues practiced in Ethiopian banking industries. The author found out that in one bank, there was a financial crime caused by an internal employee taking the advantage of sharing another person's password to undertake the crime. A phishing attack happened also in another bank of Ethiopia. In current state, many Banks do not have an overall or comprehensive IS security framework or baseline which serve as a guide to develop and implement their own Information security policy based on their own requirement in line with notional information security policy and also lack of skilled manpower (source: researcher's experience and communication with IT Security experts who work in banking industry).

In addition to the above problems the following are other indicators for the problem of security controls such as: there is no regulatory organ that supervises activities of the banks of Ethiopia regarding information security activities, there is no functional cyberspace security policy in Ethiopia [61], Security has not been given a considerable attention in Ethiopian banks, even most of the banks does not have security department or officers [59], in Ethiopia there is a lack of research in the area that can support the industries to compete with the existing technologically advanced commercial systems of the rest of the world [59]. A study in [8] have revealed that 'Information security awareness in the banking sector in Ethiopia is unsatisfactory. Consequently, the level of proper information security governance in the banking sector in Ethiopia is a critical area of improvement.

As describe under section 2.4 below the most widely used international IS Security frameworks and standards are requirement oriented, meaning that it states the requirements organizations should satisfy if they want to undergo certification in accordance with the standard [64]. In addition the majority of the research about ISMS has been performed by technologically leading countries such as the United States of America, the United Kingdom, the European Union and Australia. On top of this, information security major international standards are written from a Western perspective, without knowing how applicable ISM concepts and practices to other cultures, which has different social, organizational, and security cultures [63]. However, the standards does not mention how this can be attained. Meaning, the standard does not clearly show the steps or methods that any Bank can follow in their requirement identification process when they develop IS Security Model. The proposed IS Security model addressed this question.

Different literatures and empirical studies have revealed that information systems security domain is un-explored area, complex, whereas dramatically changed. Information Systems security challenges in banking industry are numerous and inherently diverse [8][60][61].

Information Systems security challenges in banking industry are numerous, complex, challenging and inherently diverse. Those kinds of messy situations are the objectives of this topic, which has been addressed by adopting a holistic system approach. A methodology is used that is called Soft Systems Methodology (SSM). SSM is defined by Checkland [56] as follows:

"Soft systems methodology (SSM) is an approach for tackling problematical, messy situations of all kinds. It is an action-oriented process of inquiry into problematic situations in which users learn their way from finding out about the situation, to taking action to improve it." (p. 191)

The main reasons why the author of this research adopts Soft Systems Methodology (SSM) as an approaches is to explore problem situations happened in the banks of Ethiopia and to develop IS security model. Therefore, this research adopts a broader perspective and presents an understanding of IS security in terms of a social and organizational perspective. SSM by its nature is practical, highly participative, used as a learning tool and flexible approach to manage changes by perceiving a holistic approach that takes a wider range of factors into account including social and political aspects aiming to suggest change that is meaningful and feasible in the organizational context. In addition as defined by Checkland SSM is not a system development methodology rather it is a methodology to identify changes and also it is a human problem and process oriented not technique oriented. In addition, number of models can be built to represent different viewpoints of different stakeholders and exploration of problem situations are used to decide an action for desirable changes.

From different literatures and empirical studies application of Soft Systems Methodology for developing IS security model is not implemented so far.

Taking these facts in to consideration, in this study the author of this research identify and explore IS security issues, assessed the current status and practices of IS security processes in banking industries in Ethiopia and proposed IS Security model using Soft Systems Methodology as an approach which serves as a guide for developing and implementing IS Security Baseline in bank industry in Ethiopia. Thus, the study has the following questions and objectives.

1.4 Research Questions

The research questions for this research are:

1. What are the existing IS security culture and problems in the banking industries in Ethiopia?
2. What level of IS security knowledge and awareness level does the users and top management have?
3. What are the factors that influence IS security culture practices in the banking industries in Ethiopia?
4. How better will the IS security model be developed and measured?

1.5 Objectives
1.5.1 General Objective

The general objective of this research is to develop Information Systems (IS) Security Model through Soft Systems Methodology approach for Ethiopian banking industries.

1.5.2 Specific Objectives

In order to address the general objective mentioned above the following specific objectives will be addressed.

1. Identify the existing IS security culture and problems exist in Ethiopian banking industry.
2. Identify awareness level of top management and users of the banks of Ethiopia on IS security area.
3. Identify factors that influence IS security culture practices in the banks of Ethiopia.
4. Develop IS security model using Soft System approach and measure the performance of the model.

1.6 Scope and Limitation

This research focuses on the development of IS security model using soft systems methodology approach by assessing and identifying the main issues of IS security faced in Ethiopian banks by perceiving dynamic behavior of the human aspect and holistic view of information security practices in the banking industry in Ethiopia.

This research addresses 5 banks (private and public) of Ethiopia who have full filed the criteria given by this research study. The 5 banks (branches and headquarters) are located in Addis Ababa, capital city of Ethiopia. This research uses two types of data collection techniques these are questionnaire and an interview. The primary data was collected through questionnaire (open and closed) and interview (semi-structured).

The problem that the researcher faced during the survey was getting IT managers and IT security managers since their daily operational business and meeting makes them so busy. The other problem was to get feedback on intended dates and time because of respondents' busyness and getting bored with such survey questions. There were cases where three to four visits and many phone calls were made to get responses. This could be considered as a major problem that significantly slowed down the research.

1.7 Application of Result

The result of this research will help many stakeholders of the banks of Ethiopia like:
- It will help as a guideline for those who are responsible on developing and implementing IS security policy in banks of Ethiopia.
- It enables banks of Ethiopia to have common IS security model.
- IT security staffs could be able to get a better practice and better understanding of IS security culture and the proposed model.
- Bridging the knowledge and communication gap between the top management and users of the banks of Ethiopia in IS security perspective.
- It may be an initial point for practitioners and researchers who want to conduct more comprehensive research in this area from Ethiopian banks perspective.

1.8 Ethical Consideration

During this research when data is collected from the participants by using data collecting technique (questioners and interviews), first I get a letter from my college and send these letters to the selected banks of Ethiopia to inform the managements of the banks to allow my research to be conducted in their banks. After approving the request by the management of the banks, the research is conducted. In this research:
- Everyone shall have the right to determine whether or not to participate in this research paper.

- Individuals shall not be forced to give answer to the interviews, questioners unless their free consent.
- Every research participants has the right to be informed about all aspect of the research work.
- Every respondents name shall be kept confident.

1.9 Organization of the Thesis

The thesis is organized as follow: in chapter one an introduction of information systems security and banking sectors with their related issues have been briefly discussed, define the rationale to conduct this research, discusses the statement of the problem, list the main research questions of this study, define objectives of the research, explain the scope and limitation of the research, define application of the result and finally possible ethical issues that may happen during this research and ways to avoid them are discussed.

In chapter two, an introduction and basic concepts of Soft Systems Methodology (SSM) have been briefly discussed, the basic concept of information systems security have been also discussed, history of Ethiopian banking industry is also discussed, a review of commonly used IS security framework in the world and their limitation has been discussed and a survey of previous related works that apply SSM in information systems security and information systems has been conducted and the author try to identify their limitations.

Chapter three provides the rationale for the methodology adopted for this research which is Soft Systems Methodology, the research questions, the design of the research, sampling technique, data collection technique, data analysis methods as well as designing technique and evaluation technique of the developed model are described.

In chapter four, the results of the survey are presented and has been discussed briefly. Questionnaire findings interpretations and their inferences are stated at the end of each security dimensions whereas interview findings are described in terms of words. Each interview question is presented along with a condensed text that describes each interviewee's, then a final synthesis is made that integrates these views under each question.

In chapter five, the author discusses the rationale for using SSM as an approach for this research, the result obtained from the survey is analysed following the process of SSM. Six stages of SSM are addressed and covered in this chapter (see section 5.3 – 5.5). A conceptual model is built based on the data collected from five participants. A list of recommendations that contribute to the development of systemically desirable and culturally feasible solutions is proposed.

The research is finalized in chapter six, a list of recommendations that contribute to the development of systemically desirable and culturally feasible solutions is proposed. From a strong discussion a possible specific solution is constructed for the relevant stakeholders for this research.

To generalize and to summarize chapter summaries are also provided for each chapter of this thesis except chapter one and chapter six.

CHATPTER TWO
LITERATURE REVIEW AND RELATED WORKS

2.1 Overview

This research will review a literature on an introduction and basic concepts of Soft Systems Methodology (SSM), discussing the basic concept of Information Systems Security, overview of banking industry in Ethiopia, review the most common standard used in the world, survey previous works on applying soft systems methodology in Information Systems Security and Information Systems issues.

2.2 Soft Systems Methodology (SSM)
2.2.1 Introduction

Soft Systems Methodology (SSM) was developed by Peter Checkland in the late 60's at the University of Lancaster in the UK. Originally it was seen as a modelling tool, but in later years it has been seen increasingly as a learning and meaning development tool. Although it develops models, the models are not supposed to represent the "real world", but by using systems rules and principles allow you to structure your thinking about the real world. The models are neither descriptive nor normative, though they may carry elements of both. The SSM approach stems from the 'systems movement', which Checkland see as an attempt to give holistic approaches to problems, which the traditionally reductionist approach within natural science has failed to solve. Checkland started to develop the SSM when he saw that systems engineering failed in many cases because facts and the logic of the situation never supply a complete description of a human problem situation; equally important will be the meanings by which humans make sense of their worlds. Traditional analysis focuses on the separating the individual pieces of what is being studied; in fact, the word "analysis" actually comes from the root meaning "to break into constituent parts". Whilst Systems thinking focuses on how the thing being studied interacts with the other constituents of the whole/system a set of elements that interact to produce behavior of which it is a part.

When systems practitioners bring together various systems ideas and techniques in an organized way and employ them to try to improve a problem situation, they are said to be using a 'systems methodology. Checkland in [9] tries to differentiate the two system approaches by describing soft systems approach sees organizations are complex, with problems which are "fuzzy", ill-defined, not well structured, and where multiple point of view exist where as hard system approach focus on the certain and precise situation and consider only one point of view.

SSM assumes organizational problem are 'messy', poorly defined, stakeholders interpret problems differently, human factors are important, and outcomes are learning and better understanding of problematic situation rather than a solution. As defined by Checkland SSM is not a system development methodology rather it is a methodology to identify changes and also it is a human problem and process oriented not technique oriented. A number of models can be built to represent different viewpoints of different stakeholders and exploration of problem situations are used to decide an action for desirable changes.

Soft Systems Methodology (SSM) is a systems approach that is used for analysis and problem solving in complex and messy situations. SSM uses "systems thinking" in a cycle of action research, learning and reflection to help understand the various perceptions that exist in the minds of the different people involved in the situation.

Checkland in his book [9] suggested that system analysts need to apply their skill to problems of complexity that are not well defined and that of SSM attempt to understand the wicked and fuzzy world of complex organization. This is achieved with the core paradigm of learning [10]. Therefore SSM is a systemic process of learning for exploring problem situations (systems) in an organizations for suggesting changes which will be helpful and achievable.

As defined by [11] learning is "the basic shape of the approach is to formulate some models which it is hoped will be relevant to the real-world situation, and use them by setting them against perceptions of the real world in a process of comparison. That comparison could then initiate debate leading to a decision to take purposeful action to improve the part of real life which is under scrutiny". The figure below shows the learning cycle.

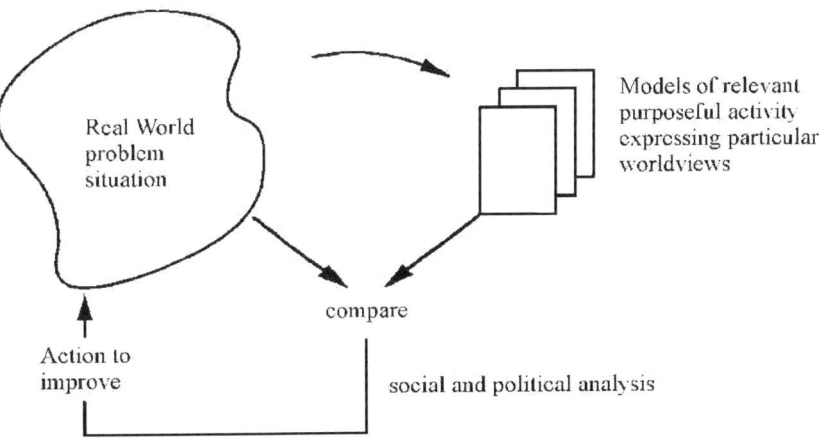

Figure 2.1 SSM as a Learning cycle (Checkland and Scholes, 1990)

The main reasons why SSM is popular from other traditional approaches is it is practical, highly participative and flexible approach to manage changes by perceiving a holistic approach that takes a wider range of factors into account including social and political aspects aiming to suggest change that is meaningful and feasible in the organizational context.

2.2.2 Seven stages of Soft Systems Methodology

Soft System Methodology have seven stages. Some of them address the "real' world, and some of address a conceptual world which is the most important part of the SSM. The figure below shows the graphical representation of seven stages of SSM.

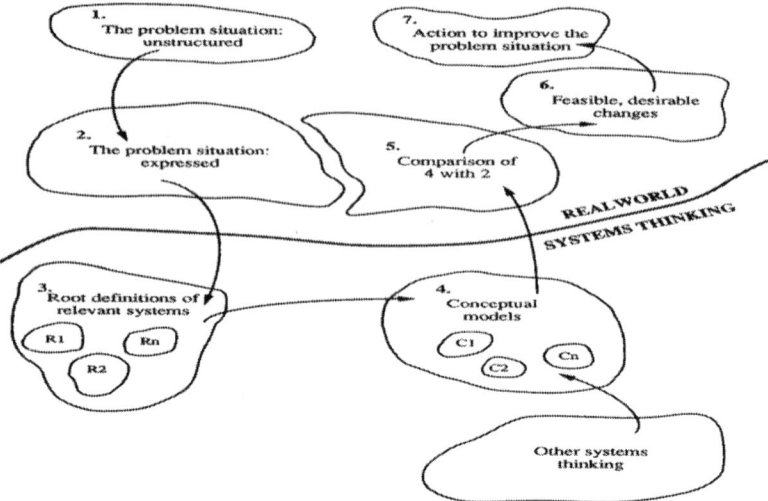

Figure 2.2 seven stages of Checkland's methodology (SSM)

Stage one: The problem situation is unstructured (ill structured)

At this stage we don't need to define the problem but asses the general area that interest us. The first step is very much in the real world problem, is to acknowledge, explore, and define the problem situation in some way to understand the "real" issues like problem owners, actors those taking part in the situation and other stakeholders. Analysts try to disclose many possible view of the situation by imagining the structure of the problem situation, activities carried out and climate in which the relationships between structure and activities.

Stage two: The problem situation is expressed

In the second stage the situation is expressed. The expression should be as rich as possible and collect as many impression as possible. Checkland in his book [26] provides some guidelines for what should be included like structures, processes, climate, people, issues expressed by people, and conflicts. Checkland suggested the best way is in pictorial form named as a rich picture. Rich picture is a graphical representation of the organization or work area. Rich picture also help to identify primary tasks that the organization must perform as part of its purpose and issues like topics, matters of concern, and conflicts.

There are some evaluation questions but not certain those are used to assure whether the rich picture is done in an appropriate way like what are the key structures, processes, climate, people, issues expressed by the people, conflicts, and how can the situation be expressed in an "unstructured" form ?

Stage three: Root Definitions of relevant system

Stage three moves out of the "real" world and enter into the world of systems. This is the Stage out of which everything else grows. That is why Checkland called it the "root definition" stage, and is the unique and most challenging part of the methodology. At this stage the first step is to understand and identify the concept of different perspectives that are possible to draw out of the rich picture that are the relevant system. A relevant system is a way of looking at the problem situation which provides useful insights.

A root definition is a short textual statements which define the important elements of the relevant system being modelled and defines who would be involved, purpose, viewpoint from which it's defined. Checkland defines root definition "**Who** is doing **what** for **whom**, to whom are they **answerable**, what **assumptions** are being made, and in what **environment**." Root definitions follow mainly the form:

A system to do X by (means of) Y in order to Z

What the system does - X
How it does it - Y
Why it's being done - Z

After that one relevant system is selected and putted through a very structured and rigorous model development process called mnemonic CATWOE developed by Checkland. The CATWOE checklist is usually used to make sure that these elements are explicitly or implicitly included. The current situation (real problem) is left behind, and the ideal situation is examined by taking systems that are relevant to the problem, then the root definition or definitions are captured by using the mnemonic **C A T W O E**. The starting point is identifying the Transformation (T).

Customer: who (what) benefits from this transformation.
Actor: who facilitates the transformation to the customers.
Transformation: the conversion of input to output (core process together with input and output).
Weltanschauung: the assumptions, the world view which makes **T** meaningful in context (rationale for the system existing).
Owner: those who pay and could stop **T** (the system).
Environment: elements outside the system that influences but does not control the system.

Stage four: Developing Conceptual Model

At this stage a conceptual model will be developed for each root definition. Conceptual model is an informal diagram of something relevant to the problematic situation, the model is not a model of problematic situation rather it is a diagram of the activities of what the system describes by the root definition will do. Conceptual models are used to structure enquiry into the problem situation, not for checking that the model matches the real world.

The process of building root definitions and conceptual models is an iterative process of debate and modification moving towards an agreed definition. There are a lots of developing a model by drawing a conceptual model using the root definition, but Checkland recommends that for beginners to follow the processes shown in the figure below:

Given: definition of T, E$_{1,2,3}$, CATWOE, Root Definition (PQR)

(1) Using verbs in the imperative ('obtain raw material X') write down activities necessary to carry out T (obtain I, transform it, dispose of Output). Aim for 7±2 activities.

(2) Select activities which could be done at once (i.e. not dependent on others):

(3) Write these out on a line, then those dependent on these first activities on a line below; continue in this fashion until all activities are accounted for. Indicate the dependencies:

(4) Redraw to avoid overlapping arrows where possible and add monitoring and control

Figure 2.3 a logical procedure for building activity model

Identify the monitor and control activities and the operational activities. A system needs control mechanisms which allow it to survive in a changing environment and to adapt to change. A monitoring and control sub-system is included in order to determine Efficiency, Effectiveness, and Efficacy of the model. These will require performance criteria to be defined for the model, and the model should provide for them to be monitored. Three types of performance measure are used in SSM these are the 3 E's:

1. Efficacy: does the means work, does it actually achieve the transformation?
2. Efficiency: does it use the minimum necessary resources?
3. Effectiveness: is the transformation meeting the longer term aim?

Stage five: Comparison of stage 4 with stage 2

In this stage a comparison of the conceptual model with the real world problematic situation has been taken place. Once the SSM practitioner has several root definitions, with accompanying conceptual model, CATWOE, and measures of performance (which together constitute rigorous and defensible conceptual systems) she/he is ready to look at the problem situation again.

Checkland suggests four ways of doing comparison
1. Unstructured discussions.
2. Structured questioning of the model using a matrix approach.
3. Scenario or dynamic modelling.
4. Trying to model the real world using the same structure as the conceptual model.

The second is the most common – often using a matrix that looks at each component of the model and asks the following questions like:

- Does it exist in the real world?
- How does it behave?
- How is its performance identified and measured?
- Is this process any good?

Stage six: Culturally Feasible and Systemically Desirable Changes

At this point the methodology tends to stop being sequential and starts swinging back and forth through all seven stages of the methodology in order to gain the greatest leverage. On the basis of this analysis possible interventions are explored.

Changes agreed upon must be **"systemically desirable"** like they must be truly relevant to the situation, and must derived from root definition and conceptual models. Changes agreed upon must be **"culturally feasible"** which means that even if it is relevant, it must consider the culture of the persons, organization and environment of which the change will be implemented.

A **consensus** is a rare special case among groups of people, and usually occurs only with respect to issues which are trivial or not contentious. Soft Systems Methodology (SSM) works with the idea of finding an **accommodation** among a group of people with a common concern. Simple or complex tabular representation can be used to show the activities in the conceptual model are set out in the left hand column, with proposed changes in the right hand column.

Stage seven: Action to improve the problem situation

The previous stages recommend action to improve the situation implement the desirable and feasible changes. Changes could be: structural, procedural, and attitudinal.

2.3. Information Systems Security

Information systems (IS) plays very important role in modern business organizations supporting its organizational efficiency or, under certain circumstances, fostering business model innovation and change. The purpose of Information Security is to protect the valuable resources of an organization such as hardware, software and skilled people. Through the selection and application of appropriate safeguard, security helps the organization to meet its business objectives or mission by protecting its physical and financial resources, reputation, legal position, employees and other tangible and intangible assets.

Information systems security protects all information assets from misuse, harm or any other unintended results by securing information, maintaining integrity of business process, retaining skilled knowledge workers with their implicit knowledge and also encouraging employees to claim ownership of their share of information assets [1]. The author also argues that "computer crime committed by internal employees is essentially a rational act" that may result from internal or external factors like personal factor, work situation and available opportunities. Crimes committed by internal employees can be either intentional or unintentional attacks. Therefore the risks posed to data by insiders need to be closely monitored and managed. The risk can be in two ways. The first one is that risk posed by malicious insiders who deliberately disclosure sensitive data for personal financial gain or other criminal purpose. The second type of risk is from insiders who unintentionally expose data. Both risks can result from carelessness or attempt to work around security measures. Information security management theorists states that the behavior of users' needs should be directed and monitored to ensure compliance with security requirements [1, 12]. This view suggests that the success of an information security depends on the user's behavior related to information security. Therefore better understanding of user's information security behaviors will assist in assessing, improving and auditing individual's information security behaviors, particularly in dynamic security environment.

Maintaining information security requires support and co-operation from all employees within the organization. Even though technical aspect of IS security needs due attention, a more serious and under-rated aspect of IS security is the human element. Reference [3] underline that the behavior of employees and their interaction with computer systems have a significant impact on the security of information. Humans are consistently referred to as the weakest link in security [13, 14]. Focus on the technical aspects of security, without due consideration of how the human interacts with the system, is clearly insufficient.

Major challenge in Information Security in banking industry is the knowledge gap about the holistic approach of Information Security Management. Due to this, most security requirements are derived by the external bodies than the Bank's management. Even though security measures are Technical, Physical and Human Banks concentrate on the technical security measures only in order to comply with the external requirements. This situation creates bad security culture [63].

Information systems security culture has a positive or negative impact in assuring information protection process in an organization. Thus, culture has influenced the formation of many security measures, such as national security policy, information ethics, security training, and privacy issues. In addition, Information Security culture covers social, cultural and ethical measures to improve the security relevant behavior of the organizational members and considered to be a subculture of organizational culture. Literature in the area of security shows that research on information security culture is still in its early stages of development. Thus, the establishment of an organizational information security culture is necessary for effective information security [63].

2.4. Commonly used IS security frameworks

In this section the author of this research discusses the most commonly used information security frameworks and standards with their limitations. There are various information security frameworks which have been widely used and applicable to banking industry such as:

FFIEC

The Federal Financial Institutions Examination Council (FFIEC) was established in 1979. It was given the authority to prescribe uniform principles, standards, and report forms for the federal examination of financial institutions. The FFIEC publication: "Information Security IT Examination Handbook" is used by federal examiners auditing the operation of financial institutions for compliance with their obligations. FFIEC's October 2005 "authentication in an internet banking environment" guidance will be part of that handbook [27].

Even if it is used as a best practice, the standard does not considers the Ethiopian culture IS security, ethical conduct of human element, the maturity level of the technology we use, and it is difficult to take it as whole to fit with ours countries financial institutions like banking industries in Ethiopia.

COBIT

Control Objectives for Information and related Technology (COBIT) is developed by the Information Systems Audit and Control Association and Foundation (ISACAF) to provide management and business process owners with an IT governance model to help understand and manage the risks associated with IT. COBIT consists of four main components namely; Plan and organize, acquire and implement, deliver and support, and finally monitor and evaluate [28].

The main focus in COBIT in addressing security is on the governance part, does not address to the main process of IS security activities. Specifically it helps for the top managements of an organisation. COBIT lacks to consider and address all the processes and other the stakeholders of the organizations staff's perception on IS security activities.

ISO 27002

The International Organization for Standardization (ISO) is "the world's largest developer and publisher of international standards in a wide area of subjects including information security management systems and practices. The ISO 27002 (2006) standard, formally the ISO 17799

(2005) standard is an industry benchmark code of practice for information security practices" [29]. IT outlines 11 control mechanisms and 130 security controls. The standard establishes guidelines and general principles for "initiating, implementing, maintaining and improving information security management within an organization" [31].

Even if ISO have so many control mechanisms, when they develop these controls they assume and considers the perception and maturity level of American and Europe peoples culture, norm and so on. And also it is not easily customizable into our organizations context.

PCI DSS

Payment Card Industry Data Security Standard is a set of comprehensive requirements for enhancing payment account data security and was developed by the founding payment brands of the PCI security standards council, including American Express, Discover Financial Services, JCB International, MasterCard Worldwide and Visa Inc. International to help facilitate the broad adoption of consistent data security measure on a global basis. The PCI DSS is a multi-faceted security standard that includes requirements for security management, policies, procedures, network architecture, software design and other critical protective measures [32].

PCI DSS security standard more relies on securing card payment transactional organizations and also doesn't consider the human aspect of IS security activities rather concentrates on the technical part of IS security.

There are some information security frameworks have been developed and widely practiced in developing countries and technologically leading countries such as United State, Australia and Europe, but each of them has its own advantages and weaknesses [33]. Commonly, it must be customized to fit with organization structure and environment [34]. Hence, this research seeks to fill the research gap. On top of this, information security major international standards are written from a Western perspective, without knowing how applicable ISM concepts and practices to other cultures, which has different social, organizational, and security cultures, (Mohammed et al., 2009). As a result, there may be a need for extra or different considerations for IS Security model Implementation in banking industry. This research conducts to fill this gap.

2.5. Brief history of Ethiopian banking industry

The history of banking in Ethiopia dates back to the era of the Axumite dynasty. However, modern banking in Ethiopia started in 1905 with the establishment of Abyssinian Bank based on a 50 years agreement with the Anglo-Egyptian National Bank. In 1908 a new development bank (named Societe Nationaled'Ethiope Pour le Development de l'Agriculture et du Commerce) and two other foreign banks (Banque de l'Indochine and the Compagnie de l'Afrique Oreintale) were also established cited in [35]. These banks were criticized for being wholly foreign owned. In 1931 the Ethiopian government purchased the Abyssinian Bank, which was the dominant bank, and renamed it the Bank of Ethiopia'– the first nationally owned bank on African continent [36].

In 1943 the Ethiopian government has established its own bank called State Bank of Ethiopia, which was serving both the commercial bank and central bank activities. Later on it is further dissolved into today's National Bank of Ethiopia (NBE) and Commercial Bank of Ethiopia (CBE). Before the Derg regime (1974 through1991), there were private and state owned banks operating in the country such as CBE, AIDB (DBE), and HSB (CBB). By then, all financial institutions including banks were nationalized.

After 1992 (the fallen Derg regime) the financial sector has been deregulated that gives birth to private banks, insurance companies and micro finance institutions. Recently, the number of banks operating in the country reached 18 of which 2 of them are owned by the state and the remaining 16 are private commercial banks.

In general, there were five major proceedings has been occur in Ethiopian banking sector history regarded to Ethiopian political instability since 1905 are:

- The first event was, 1906, when, the establishment of the Bank of Abyssinia, marking the advent of banking into the country.
- The second event was Italian invasion in 1936, after liquidation of the Bank of Ethiopia, control a colonial banking network.
- The third event was the establishment of State Bank of Ethiopia in 1943, marking the rebirth of the Ethiopian independent banking.
- The fourth event was the revolution of 1974, which wiped out the monarchy, nationalized companies and the whole credit system being based on the central bank and three state owned financial institutions.
- The fifth event was, 1991, the collapse of socialist regime followed by a financial sector reform and liberalization.

2.6 Related Works

This research conduct a literature review aiming to explore and assess related works and previous studies on Information Systems security and application of Soft Systems Methodology (SSM).

A work in [17] outlines a successful mission of how to bridge the gap between general management and ICT technicians. It is based on practical experience obtained from an ongoing study which aims at developing guidelines for managing ICT security in organizations generally. The study was initially conducted in five organizations in Tanzania in order to make preliminary observations. Later one organization was earmarked as a test-bed for further observations. The study was guided by using the Business Requirements on Information Technology Security (BRITS) framework used together with Security by Consensus (SBC) model. The main objective of this research is to bridge the gap between the management and the technical department was achieved through the proposed 10 steps. The CEO buying into the idea first; recognizing that the technical departments are the custodians of ICT in the organization; starting it as a special project; showing where the risks and their consequences are; getting the entire management's attention; taking stock of the existing situation; conducting awareness-raising sessions to address the ICT security problem with respect to the organization's specific environment; carrying out detailed risk assessment; working out a short-term plan for issues that need immediate attention and a long-term plan to finally develop the countermeasures for the identified problems. However the proposed guideline fails to consider other stakeholders (employees) of the organization, it only considers and addresses the top management and technical personnel's of the organization.

Reference [18] tries to develop and propose specific Information Security Governance Framework (ISGF) for governing the information security with banking environment and information technology or information system in mind. The main concern of the researcher to develop the framework are the threats and security breaches that are highly increasing in recent years in the world, the insiders and outsider attacks that have caused global business lost in trillions of dollars in each year. The framework is categorized into three levels which are Strategic level, Tactical and Operational level, and Technical level. The study showed that a comprehensive information security governance framework highly needed for banking information system. Some general standards and best practices have been developed, but none of them can fulfill specific and unique needs of an organization. This in-progress research is to develop a specific information security governance framework within the banking environment and IT/IS in mind. The framework can be used as an initial effort for bank to govern their information security. The framework is an integration of all framework components available today. Essentially, the framework is still a general approach to information security governance program, it needs to be reviewed by professionals and comprehensively tested in the real banking environment.

Another work [19] focuses on the effect of strong corporate cultures and organizational commitment as important aspects for enhancing information security. The research tries to examine the extent to which information security behaviors, as part of an organizational culture, relate to a common work attitude variable known as organizational commitment. The authors prepare an anonymous survey questioner for Two hundred and twenty seven (93 women and 134 men) employees of a large sized bank in Greece took part in the survey. After the survey the authors try to conclude that in order to ensure effective and proactive information security, all staff must be active participants rather than passive observers of information security. In doing so, staff must strongly held and widely share the norms and values of the organizational culture in terms of information security perception. A well-established culture and well trained end-users can address the security planning and management of information within an organization. However in research [19] there is no model, guideline, or framework to be followed or practiced.

The main objective of the research [20] is to demonstrate the application of Soft System Methodology (SSM) to issues and obstacles facing Saudi Arabian government organizations using information and computer technology (ICT). A number of techniques and approaches were used in achieving these objectives including quantitative and qualitative techniques of data analysis. An empirical study indicates that most subject organizations suffer from people issues rather than technical issues. By applying SSM, the study identified the problems and obstacles facing Saudi government organizations. At last a conceptual model has been proposed. Even if the approach used in the research [20] is useful for the research I am conducting, but the proposed model is directly applicable for the Information Communication Technology issues and problems which does not specifically address the information security aspects.

The main concern of the work [21] is to apply Soft Systems Methodology (SSM) in evaluating the Nigerian Tourism industry and offered solutions. The main concern of this research was: Low level of demand mainly caused by poor perception of tourism in Nigeria; Inadequate publicity and negative media reports; Inadequate measures to attract private investors; Poor infrastructure/Insufficient tourism facilities; Poor manpower; Problem of land acquisition; Poor management information systems; Apathy of many Nigerians toward tourism; Security risk and Economic instability. In this study I have learned that how SSM is used but the topic is totally different with my research topic, which means the approach is useful for my research but the content is different with my topic.

In the study [37] Soft Systems Methodology is used as a diagnostic tool to analyze a real case information security incident. The increasing complexity of current security breaches happened all over the world are the main reasons in which the research is conducted. The authors use qualitative methodology to collect data by conducting unstructured interview. In this study the approach (SSM) is useful for the research I am conducting, but the content is like they used SSM as a diagnostic tool to analyze a real case information security incident not used to propose the a comprehensive information security conceptual model. Therefore, my research is to fill this gap, which is to propose information systems security conceptual model.

One of the related works done was on "Information Security Culture in the banking sector in Ethiopia" by [8]. The purpose of this study was to investigate the extent the information security culture of Ethiopia and indicated that, even big banks in the world that generally do better job of security are found to be victims of security breaches. Finally the authors recommended that there is also a significant space to enhance the trust environment between manager and employees that can promote change in information security culture and more rigorous researches are needed to frame practical strategies to enhance the information security culture in the banking sectors in Ethiopia [8]. Therefore, the focus of the research was on the assessment of security culture in Ethiopia. Even if one the specific objectives of my research is assessing information systems security culture of the Ethiopian banking industry, the main objectives of my research is developing Information Systems Security Model using SSM approach in case of Ethiopian banking industry.

The main objective of the work by Shemlse Gebremedhin [57] is to propose applicable information systems security auditing framework to support people in the area of IT Auditing. Due to lack of professionals and adequate frameworks in the area the information systems security audit issues is getting scaled up to become a severe problem. This study has been conducted on the Ethiopian banking industry using mixed research method as a research paradigm and survey questionnaire and interview are used as a method of data collection. The developed security concept on the ontology has been properly defined and related in hierarchical structure base. Finally, different templates and models were prepared to identify, assess and to measure security concepts quantitatively. The overall IS security audit activity is proposed to be performed by eight audit processes which have been explicitly stated in the framework. Finally, the researcher propose future work to develop and implement information systems security audit framework for organizations other than bank. Even if the research [57] stands by perceiving IS security issues that exists in Ethiopian banking industry and assuming the complexity of IS security activities of Ethiopian banks, the research mainly focuses on developing information systems security audit framework for the respected banks of Ethiopia. However, my research objectives is to see a holistic view of IS security issues and problems that exists in Ethiopian banking industry and to develop IS security model in order to propose possible solution for improving IS security processes and activities of Ethiopian banks. Besides SSM helps the author of this research to see IS security in a holistic view rather than specific part of IS security.

Another related work by Aychiluhim Desisa [58] was to develop and propose internet banking security framework. In this research questionnaire and interview have been conducted in order to gather data from different number of experts from the field of security, network, e-payment, risk and compliances aims to find potential security improvements of internet banking system in Ethiopian banking industry. This research finds that the critical way of internet banking fraud is one way or another is social engineering attacks. This emanated from the client's side security loop holes. To overcome the major security issues, the research resulted to design internet banking security framework and its major five models under two major layers such as inner and outer layers that constitute holistic multiple layered security insured. Internet banking security framework and its major five models have been developed and evaluated through expert evaluation method. The research [58] main objectives was to develop internet banking security framework and its major five models aiming to overcome the majority security issues specifically for social engineering attacks. However, security breaches and incidents are not only social engineering attacks, there are variety of attacks, incidents, issues and problems that needs to be considered as IS security issues and problems. Therefore, my research aim is to fill the abovementioned gaps by perceiving a holistic view of IS security issues that exists in Ethiopian banking industry and to develop a comprehensive IS security model using Soft Systems Methodology as an approach.

The author of this research summarized the related works in to table format as shown in the table below.

Table 2.1 Summary of related works

	Author's name and year	Objectives of the work	Methods and techniques	Key findings
1.	Jabiri K. Bakari, Charles N. Tarino, Louise Yngstrom, Christer Magnusson, and Stewart Kowalski	To bridge the gap between the management and the technical department through the 10 proposed steps	The research is based on practical experience obtained from an ongoing study. The study was guided by using the Business Requirements on Information Technology Security (BRITS) framework used together with Security by Consensus (SBC) model.	10 proposed steps such as: The CEO buying into the idea first; recognizing that the technical departments are the custodians of ICT in the organization; starting it as a special project; showing where the risks and their consequences are; getting the entire management's attention; taking stock of the existing situation; conducting awareness-raising sessions to address the ICT security problem with respect to the organization's specific environment; carrying out detailed risk assessment; working out a short-term plan for issues that need immediate attention and a long-term plan to finally develop the countermeasures for the identified problems.
2.	Munirul Ula, Zurain bt Ismail, and Zailani M. Sidek	To develop and propose specific Information Security Governance Framework (ISGF) for governing the information security with banking environment and information technology or information system in mind.	Reviewing the literatures, and comparing the commonly used approaches to information security governance frameworks in order to define and construct new information security governance for banking	An Information Security Governance framework is developed. The proposed framework is categorized into three levels which are Strategic level, Tactical, and Operational level, and Technical level.
3.	Ioannis Koskosas, Konstantinos Kakoulidis, Christos Siomos	To examine the extent to which information security behaviors, as part of an organizational culture, relate to a common work attitude variable known as organizational commitment.	This research uses a quantitative research method. The authors prepare an anonymous questionnaire.	The authors concluded that in order to ensure effective and proactive information security, all staff must be active participants rather than passive observers of information security.

4.	Saleh Al-Zhrani	To demonstrate the application of SSM to issues and obstacles facing Saudi government organizations attempting to manage ICT to their advantage.	This research uses both quantitative and qualitative techniques of data analysis.	By applying SSM, a conceptual framework is developed and proposed in order to identify ICT problems in Saudi public organizations.
5.	Bilal AlSabbagh, Stewart Kowalski	To demonstrate how the methodology (SSM) can be considered a beneficial tool for security analysts during security incident management and risk analysis.	Real case experiment and The authors use qualitative methodology to collect data by conducting unstructured interview.	SSM is applied as a framework to diagnose a real case security incident in an organization.
6.	Umoh, Godwin I. and Ndu Eugene C.	Applying SSM to evaluate Nigerian Tourism Industry and proffered solution.	Real case experiment on Nigerian Tourism sector.	
7.	Abiy. W and Lemma. L, August 20, 2012	To investigate the extent of information security culture of Ethiopia.	A survey method which is (questionnaire) is used to assess IS security culture in Ethiopian banks.	There is a significant space to enhance the trust environment between the manger and employees that can promote change in information security culture of Ethiopian banking industry.
8.	Shemlse G/Medhin Kassa July 2013	To develop information systems security audit framework.	Mixed research method is used as a research paradigm and survey questionnaire and interview are used as a method of data collection	Different templated and models were prepared to identify, asses and to measure security concepts quantitatively. Eight audit processes have been proposed.
9.	Aychiluhim Desisa May 2014	To design internet banking security framework and its major five models.	Questionnaire and in-depth interview have been conducted in order to gather data.	Internet banking framework and its five major models have been designed under two layers such as: Inner and outer layer that establish multiple layered security ensured.

2.7 Summary

Information security management theorists states that the behavior of users' needs should be directed and monitored to ensure compliance with security requirements [1, 12]. This view suggests that the success of an information security depends on the user's behavior related to information security. Therefore better understanding of user's information security behaviors will assist in assessing, improving and auditing individual's information security behaviors, particularly in dynamic security environment.

Concept behind Information Systems security, systems thinking and soft systems methodology as well as the seven stages has been discussed in the literature review. And also a brief history of Ethiopian banking industry has been discussed in the literature review. In addition the author of this research discussed their contribution and limitation of the commonly used IS security and frameworks and standards in the world.

Related works such as recommending a solution to bridge the gap between the management and the technical department on IS security, developing and proposing IS security governance, examining the extent of IS security in organizational culture, demonstrating the application of SSM to issues and obstacles in the organization, applying SSM as a diagnose tool for security incident management analysis and applying SSM to evaluate the proffered solution or framework of the organization studied and reviewed in depth.

CHAPTER THREE
METHODOLOGY

3.1 Overview

This research has an overview on the activities of methodology such as define how and why the research is designed, presenting what type of sampling technique is used with justification, identify and explain the type of data collection techniques used in this research, explain how the data's are analyzed, highlight how the proposed model is designed and explains how the proposed model is evaluated.

3.2 Research Design

A research design is a plan, structure and strategy of investigation so conceived as to obtain answers to research questions or problems. The plan is the complete scheme or program of the research. It includes an outlines of what the investigator will do from writing the hypothesis and their operational implication to the final analysis of the data [22].

This research is a mixed methodology. Mixed methodology research is the type of research in which the researcher mixes or combines qualitative and quantitative research philosophies or paradigms, methodologies, methods, techniques, approaches, concepts, or language into a single research study or a set of related studies. Mixed methodology research refers to the combination of quantitative and qualitative research [23] and its basic principle is that the combination provides a better understanding of research problems than either approach by itself [24]. [25] Suggest that this approach is both a methodology and a method.

3.3 Sampling technique and sampling design

The researcher used the following sampling components: population, sampling method, and sample frame and sample size to prepare sampling design.

3.3.1 Source of data

The primary data sources used in this research are non-technical staffs, IS/IT staffs including Managers and Directors and IS security experts including managers who have direct or indirect relationships on/to IS security processes and activities.

3.3.2 Population

The population of the study was five banks (branches and Headquarters) in Addis Ababa and the researcher collected 5 (five) banks' data. The population of the 5 selected bank is 6,610 staffs. The population of the surveyed banks are described in a table format as shown below.

Table 2.2 summary of the population of surveyed banks

Bank	Bank type	population size in Addis Ababa (relevant to this research only)	Participant's role
1	Public	2960	IT department directors and Managers, IT department staffs and non-technical staffs (branch and head quarter staffs)
2	Private	1000	IT department directors and Managers, IT department staffs and non-technical staffs (branch and head quarter staffs)
3	Private	900	IT department directors and Managers, IT department staffs and non-technical staffs (branch and head quarter staffs)
4	Public	250	IT department directors and Managers, IT department staffs and non-technical staffs (branch and head quarter staffs)
5	Private	1500	IT department directors and Managers, IT department staffs and non-technical staffs (branch and head quarter staffs)
Total number of population		6,610	

3.3.3 Sampling method

This study employed a Non-probability sampling method. Initially purposive sampling was used to select sample banks out of eighteen Ethiopian banks. The sampling criteria for this research is banks having information security office or at least having information security manager and senior information security officer. The main reason to use such kind of criteria is because if the IS security office or division is not established in the bank, the information security practices of the bank will not be efficient and effective for investigating the research and implementing the framework. Without the responsible information security office or information security division the proposed IS security framework will not be applicable. Therefore five banks (Abyssinia, Dashen, Wegagen, Commercial Bank of Ethiopia and Development Bank of Ethiopia) full filed the criteria from all 18 banks of Ethiopia. Three banks (Abyssinia, Dashen, and Wegagen) are private banks and two banks (Commercial Bank Ethiopia, Development Bank of Ethiopia) are governmental banks of Ethiopia.

The author of this research used the quota sampling technique; as such it is a Non-probability sample method for questionnaires purpose in all sample public and private banks. The researcher distributes 150 questionnaires for the 5 surveyed banks of Ethiopia. The researcher distributes the questionnaire by himself. The researcher chooses to give 30 questionnaires for 30 participants for one bank and selects three participant group which are 5 questionnaires for IT department directors and managers, 10 questionnaire for IT department staffs and 15 questionnaire for non-technical staffs of the bank. The distribution mechanism is the same through the five surveyed banks of Ethiopia.

The sampling method used for the interview was purposive sampling technique. Purposive sampling refers to situations where participants are selected based on their specialized insight or special perspective, experience, characteristic, or condition when there is something the researcher wishes to get and understand [38].

The author of this research also used a purposive sampling technique in order to select 5 IT security Managers from each selected banks for the purpose of using the approach (Soft Systems Methodology) in order to conduct an un-structured interview for discussion to come up with an agreed or accommodation of a well-constructed Rich picture of the expressed problem situation and to establish a possible changes which are desirable and feasible.

3.3.4 Sample scope

Sampling scope refers to a list or set of direction that identifies the target population. Thus, the target population of this study is those 5 selected Banks. The selected banks of Ethiopia were: Commercial Bank of Ethiopia (CBE), Dashen Bank S.C. (DB), Wegagen Bank S.C. (WB), Development Bank of Ethiopia (DBE), and Abyssinia Bank S.C. (AB). These banks were selected by purposive sampling method.

3.3.5 Sample size

The sample size of this study is 5 banks in which the population size is 6,610 staffs of the surveyed banks of Ethiopia. This means 27.8 % of the total population ((5/18)*100%). The technique was used to get data from the banks of Ethiopia by using data collection techniques. In this research 150 questioners were distributed to the selected banks of Ethiopia to non-technical staffs (branch staffs and head office staffs) and IT department staff in order to get information on information security culture, knowledge level and communication gap of the staffs of each selected banks of Ethiopia. The interview was conducted to 15 persons (5 information security manager, 5 senior information security officer, and 5 IT/IS Directors) of the selected banks of Ethiopia in order to get a greater understanding of IS security problem that is currently facing in their banks.

On the other hand, the author of this research conduct un-structured interview for the 5 IT security managers and conduct a discussion to construct a rich picture to the express the problem situation clearly using the approach or Soft Systems Methodology (SSM).

3.4 Data Collection Technique

This research uses concurrent embedded data collection strategy or design. Concurrent mixed method data collection strategies have been employed to validate one form of data with the other form, to transform the data for comparison, or to address different types of questions [25]. Concurrent embedded data collection strategy or design has two purposes, the primary purpose of the design is to gain a broader perspective than could be gained from using only the predominant data collection method and the secondary purpose is use of embedded method to address different research questions or to gather information from different groups or levels within an organization.

This research uses two types of data collection techniques these are questionnaire and an interview. The primary data was collected through questionnaire (open and closed) and interview (semi-structured and un-structured interview for the discussion).

3.4.1 Questionnaires

Questionnaire is one of the most common type of instrument to conduct a quantitative research methods. The questionnaires were distributed to the employees of the selected banks of Ethiopia. The questions were designed to ask a response on the participant's perception of risk for certain activities (perceived value), their perception of risk behavior (culture), their perception while others committing to security activities (commitment), their perception of information security culture with in the bank, knowledge of the participant's on IS security area. This will help us in finding the knowledge gap in IS security practices and existing IS security culture of the banks.

The author of this research used an existing information security culture assessment questionnaire [39] as a starting point to design the questionnaire for this empirical study and enhances the questionnaire by customizing and adding some statements and add categories in the existing questionnaire in a way to be suitable for the respondents knowledge, attitude, perception and culture. The existing questionnaire is based on the framework developed by Martin and Eloff for information security culture in the work [39]. It assisted the researcher of this study to use statements that related to the dimensions of IS security culture. Martin and Eloff used a similar approach to conduct the survey and therefore it was possible to use the questionnaire in the context of this research. The content of the questionnaire is document at the end of this document as **Appendix A.**

The questionnaire is divided into four sections such as Knowledge statement, IS security culture statement, Biographical question, and General statement. The questions items are structured on humans knowledge on IS security practices and status on IS Security culture of the banks of Ethiopia. The questioners were distributed to IT/IS manager/Directors, IT staffs, Non-technical staffs (such as customer service officers, risk department staffs, HR officers etc.) of the respective sampled banks. The questionnaire had 53 questions in four sections. The first sections is biographical questions are added in the questionnaire to segment the data and comparisons within the population. The second section is included to determine how much knowledge employees have about IS security. The third section assess the perception of employees about the six Information Security Culture Framework component categories, the remaining one component category of the ISCF is not used in this study due to acceptable reason which is described in the next chapter. And the fourth section deals with the general opinion of employees on using IT related things with respect of IS security.

3.4.2 Interview

Informal information about interviewees experience and knowledge has been collected by the researcher before conducting an interview. They possess the experience and perspective in IS security culture and practices in which this research wishes to understand. Given the security management experience and background of potential interviewees, purposive sampling method seems the most logical choice for data collection [40].

Interview is the most relevant and common type in order to conduct qualitative research methods. In this research an interview is conducted in order to get an in-depth and a greater understanding of the main problems of IS security in the selected banks of Ethiopia. The interview used in this research is a semi-structured interview. The interview addresses total of 15 persons (5 information security managers, 5 senior information security officers, and 5 IT/IS directors) of the selected banks of Ethiopia.

The main purpose of this interview meeting is to complement and increase the validity and reliability of the information obtained through the questionnaire. The following points were addressed. Questions about Information Systems Security Framework development and implementation practice are conducted. Interview questions used in this research are attached at the end of this document as **Appendix B**.

In addition to the above interview the student researcher also conduct un-structured interview for discussion with the selected 5 IT security managers for the purpose of constructing a rich picture to express the problem situation using the approach (SSM).

The appointment was given to interviewees approximately 3 days before their scheduled interview date due to the busyness of the interviewees specially IT/IS directors and IT/IS security managers. The average time for the interviews was 1 hour. All interviews were conducted face-to-face, in person, at the interviewees' site of business.

3.5 Pilot Study

In order to assess the significance of the instruments designed to collect data for the study, the pilot study was conducted in one of the sample Banks for 15 staffs (1 IT director, 2 IT managers, 5 IT department staffs and 7 non-technical staffs). The aim was to find out and avoid ambiguity, omissions and misunderstanding of each item. Using the relevant comments from results of the pilot study and suggestions of the advisor corrections was made. Some of the changes that have been made are: The multiple choices and open ended questions were added in order to perceive the employee opinion on the general IT related operation with respect to security. Further the number of questions reduced to 53. Moreover, correcting some vague questions was made.

3.6 Procedures

The data-gathering tool used in the study was drafted on the basis of the reviewed literature and the intended data to be collected. The set of questionnaires were distributed to the respondents. The data collection process was administrated by the student researcher. All interviews have been done by the student researcher. Data collections through interview were conducted by speaking to the respondents face to face. Before conducting the interview, the student researcher has tried to create conducive atmosphere and explain the purpose of the interview to them. As a result necessary information was collected, organized and processed separately for interpreting and summarizing purpose to produce the major findings. By integrating and combining the survey results (questionnaire and interview findings) with the "rich picture" obtained from the key stakeholders by using the approach (SSM), finally the student researcher develop and propose Information Systems security framework by using Soft System Approach.

3.7 Data Analysis Technique

Data analysis method for this research follows SSM with the integration of concurrent embedded design of data analysis technique for the combination of qualitative and quantitative data. The questionnaire (quantitative data) were analyzed by quantitative data analysis technique (descriptive statistics) and the interview (qualitative data) were analyzed by qualitative data analysis technique (observation while interviewing). By combining the analyzed survey data's (questionnaire and interview findings) by combining with the rich picture drawn by the author of this research using Soft Systems Methodology (SSM) for further analysis and for conceptual model development. The details of analysis stages were described on the next chapter.

After the collecting of raw data, classification and tabulation was done by the researcher to make it ready for the analysis. Some of the collected data's were organized and processed separately for each item questions and some of them were grouped in a way appropriate to answer the research questions raised in this research. Descriptive statistics was used to analyze the data by employing SPSS statistics version 20 software. In addition to this statistical tool like charts, and verbal descriptions was used to present the data.

In addition to the above data analysis the problem situation is analysed and expressed in what we call "Rich picture" using the approach called soft systems methodology (SSM) in order to identify the social, cultural and political issues, concerns and conflicts of the dynamic nature of the human activities and organizational activities is also undertaken in chapter 5.

3.8 Design Technique

An Information Systems security framework that takes the research findings of earlier steps as an input was designed using seven stages of Soft System approach. The layout of designing the framework using seven stages of Soft System approach is shown in the figure below.

```
                          Start
                   ↓              ↓
     Rich Picture              Summary of the survey
 Problem situation expressed:   (Questionnaire and Interview findings)
       stage 1&2
                   ↓
        Root Definition of relevant systems: stage 3
                   ↓
        Develop conceptual model (IS Security Framework): stage 4
                   ↓
                        Evaluation
 (Comparison of the model with the rich picture and summary of the survey): stage 5
                   ↓
 Develop suggested changes (systematically desirable and culturally feasible): stage 6
                   ↓
                          End
```

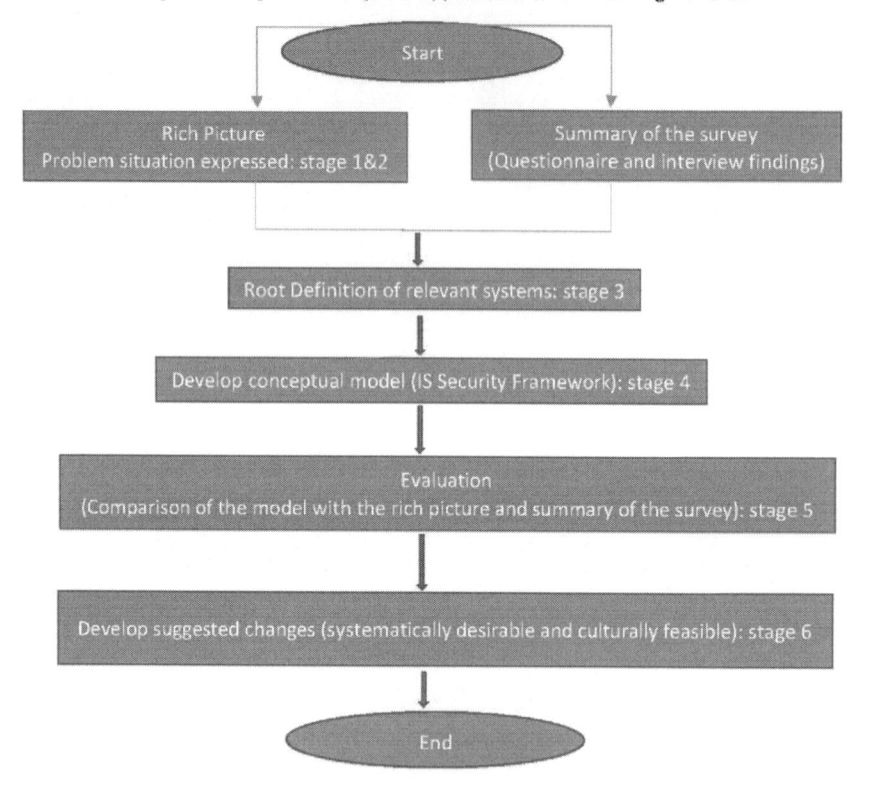

Figure 3.1 the general layout for developing the model (IS security Model)

3.9 Evaluation Technique

The proposed IS Security Model was evaluated by professionals (domain experts) by conducting an interview and advanced based on the sound comments and suggestions. The content of the interview question is presented at the end of the document as *Appendix C*.

3.10 Summary

This research adopts a combination of quantitative and qualitative research methodology named as mixed methodology. Quantitative data collection technique which is the questionnaire is distributed to 150 participants of the surveyed banks to get a response on the participant's perception, culture, commitment, knowledge and awareness level on IS security area. The other data collection technique is an interview that is used to get an in-depth and a greater understanding of the main problems and issues of IS security in the surveyed banks of Ethiopia. The primary data was collected through questionnaire (open and closed) and interview (semi-structured and un-structured). On the other hand the problem situation is analysed and expressed by constructing rich picture by using the approach (Soft Systems Methodology).

The author of this research tries to explain how the sample populations are selected, what kind of sampling method he choose to use and why, and describes who are the sample, why he choose how he addresses the sample population and try to explain to what extent this research is.

The research also uses concurrent embedded design of data analysis technique for quantitative and qualitative data obtained from both quantitative and qualitative data collection technique. After the collecting of raw data, classification and tabulation was done by the researcher to make it ready for the analysis. Some of the collected data's were organized and processed separately for each item questions and some of them were grouped in a way appropriate to answer the research questions raised in this research. Descriptive statistics was used to analyze the data by employing SPSS statistics version 20 software. In addition to this statistical tool like charts, and verbal descriptions was used to present the data.

At last the author of this research demonstrates how the conceptual model is going to be developed and highlights how the developed model is evaluated.

CHAPTER FOUR
FINDINGS INTERPRETATON AND INFERENCES

4.1 Overview

In this section findings of the study and its interpretations are presented under each question items whereas implications are stated at the end of each security dimension. The aim of the field study is to discover the state of the information system security practice of banks involved in financial services to the people using IT. Questionnaires and interview questions were used as instrument to carry out the study. The questionnaires were used to collect data about IS security culture and knowledge of employees on IS security area and the student researcher own additional points which are relevant to inspect IS security culture and knowledge of employees on IS security practice in the banking industry. The summary of the findings of each question item under each dimension in the surveyed banks is attached at the end as *Appendix E*.

This study research findings are classified into two major areas such as; findings from the interviews and findings from questionnaires. Questionnaire findings provided insight into the knowledge of employees on IS security area and how IS security culture is practiced in the surveyed banks. Findings from Interview clarified the general issues in information security in addition to supplement the questionnaires.

4.2 Respondent Information

The respondents of the research include Non IT staffs such HR officers, financial experts, Risk officers, Customer Service Officers who are directly use and operate the core banking system, IT staffs who are engaged in managerial position and decision maker about IT security. The job title of these officials are IT/IS director/Managers, IT staffs, and Non-technical staffs.

4.3 Data collection procedure using questionnaire

The questionnaire was given to IT staffs and Non-technical staffs such HR officers, financial experts, Risk officers, Customer Service Officers etc. in one of the sampled bank as a means of testing whether the questions were easily understood. After accommodating recommendations from these groups of people and my adviser, the questionnaires were personally distributed to the banks listed in section 4.2. And then the student researcher has collected the filled questionnaires. The questionnaires are attached as an *Appendix A* at the end of this document.

Cooperation letter which was written by Hilcoe College and introductory statement about privacy of respondents is a document which is attached to a survey questionnaire in order to raise the motivation of the respondents and to create comfort zone. This is used as a guarantee that the information provided is to be used only for the stated purpose.

The survey was carried out in 5 Ethiopian banks from November 05 - 25, 2016. The survey was done in person to increase the response rate and also succeed in the study even though it is time taking to get responses from a given bank.

4.4 Response rate

When a validity test is conducted, the commonly accepted criterion is to have at least 100 respondents or five times the number of responses compared to the number of questions in the assessment instrument [41]. 129 questionnaires were collected from the 5 banks in which 150 questionnaire were distributed. Therefore, the response rate is 86% calculated using:

Number of completed questionnaire = $\frac{129}{150}$ *100 = 0.86 X 100= 86%
Number of questionnaire sent out

This shows that the response rate is high and it could be considered valid for proceeding with the analysis of data obtained.

4.5 Findings
4.5.1 Questionnaire findings

In this section, the results from data analysis are presented and addressing the main components of Information Security Culture Framework (ISCF) which make up the themes .The data analysis result is depicted using charts in percentage which refers to the number of banks having or not having certain IS security culture and employees knowledge on IS security areas. As has been indicated in section 4.2 (response) above, the result of the analysis is based on the responses obtained from 5 banks. For the sake of simplicity findings of the knowledge statement questionnaire was summarized and attached as an *appendix D* at the end of this document.

All the statements are categorized in to six dimensions based on the ISCF [42]. The components were Leadership and governance dimension, Security management and organization dimension, security program management dimension, User security management dimension, Technology protection and operation dimension, and Change dimension.

SPSS was used to compile different reports in order to interpret the empirical study results. The mean, percentage favorable, neural (undecided) and unfavorable responses for each statement were analyzed. To obtain the percentage for favorable responses, the strongly agree and agree responses were grouped together. The strongly disagree and disagree responses were also grouped together to institute the percentage of unfavorable responses. This was done to represent the result in a more easily understandable format for the selected banks of Ethiopia.

For the sake of simplicity the respondents job status is categorized in to three parts such as from total respondents 23.3% respondents are IT staffs, 69.8% are Non-technical staffs such as such HR officers, financial experts, Risk officers, Customer Service Officers etc., and 7.0% are IT/IS

Directors/Managers (see table 4.1). The largest number of respondents had worked for the bank for between one and three years (39.5%), between four and five years (24.8%), between six and ten years (21.7%) and the rest of the respondents had worked for more than ten years (14.0%) (See table 4.2). Most of the respondents educational background is Degree (86.8%), and the rest of the respondents are Diploma (6.2%) and Masters (7.0%) educational background (see table 4.3).

Table 4.1 summary of job status

1. your job			
		Frequency	Percent
Job Status	IT Staffs	30	23.3%
	Non-IT Staffs	90	69.8%
	IT/IS Directors/Managers	9	7.0%
	Count	129	100.0%

Table 4.2 summary of length of service in the bank

2. Length of service in the bank			
		Frequency	Percent
Length of Service in the Bank	1 to 3 Years	51	39.5%
	4 to 5 Years	32	24.8%
	6 to 10 Years	28	21.7%
	More than 10 Years	18	14.0%
	Count	129	100.0%

Table 4.3 summary of educational background

3. your educational background			
		Frequency	Percent
Educational Background	Certificate	0	0.0%
	Diploma	8	6.2%
	Degree	112	86.8%
	Masters	9	7.0%
	Others	0	0.0%
	Count	129	100.0%

The knowledge questions were analysed separately from the culture questions, as these two groups of questions each had different objectives. The knowledge questions are used to provide background in analysing the culture questions and they focus what employees "know". The IS security culture questions are used to measure the level of IS security culture in the bank and focus on the opinion and perception of employees regarding the information security components defined in the Information Security Culture Framework (ISCF).

The next few paragraphs provide an overview of the results of the knowledge and IS security culture statements, as well as the key recommendations.

Figure 4.1 below shows that graphical representation (bar chart) of the respondents who select "Yes" with their percentage figures. From the result it is evident that most of the employees (67.44%) are aware of the banks information security policy, but 58.9% does not know where to obtain a copy. Because of that reason 48.8% of the employees could not read the information security policy sections that are applicable to their jobs. 36.43% of employees are not informed of security requirements to protect information. Most of the employees (71.3%) do not take adequate information security awareness training. A total of 59.7% employees do know how to use the anti-virus software to scan for viruses. The reason for this could be that the bank configured the anti-virus software to automatically scan for viruses. The overall awareness average 66.77% of the total employees are aware of information security knowledge which needs a little bit improvement.

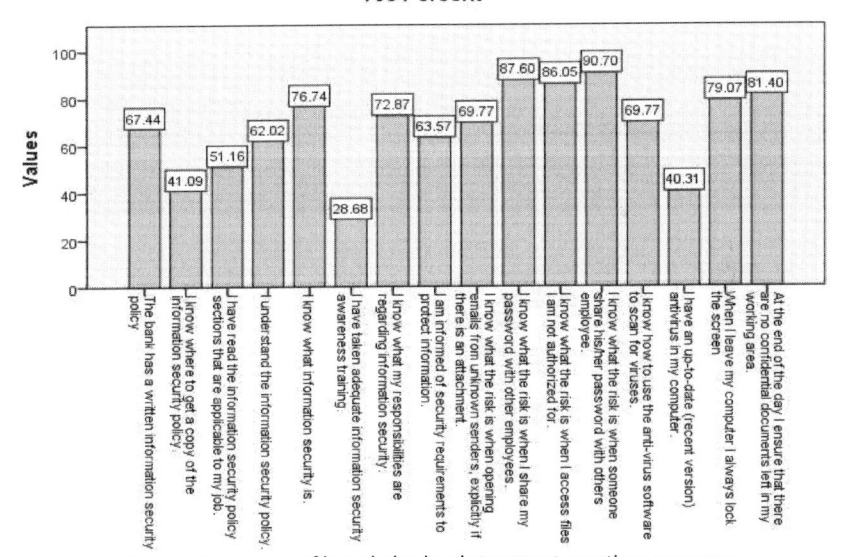

Figure 4.1 summary of knowledge level statement questions response

Table 4.4 below shows the overall results of the six information security culture dimensions. The two dimensions were the employees perception where the most unfavorable or negative dimension were User Security Management and Technology Protection. Security Program Management and were the most favorable or positive dimensions.

Table 4.4 summary result of the six information security culture dimensions

Dimensions	Unfavorable		Undecided		Favorable		Total	
	Count	Percent	Count	Percent	Count	Percent	Count	Percent
Leadership and Governance	125	19.40%	158	24.50%	362	56.10%	645	100.0%
Security Management and Organization	73	18.90%	104	26.90%	210	54.30%	387	100.0%
Security Program Management	50	12.90%	96	24.80%	241	62.30%	387	100.0%
User Security Management	335	23.6%	276	19.7%	805	56.7%	1419	100.0%
Technology Protection	212	23.5%	251	27.8%	440	48.7%	903	100.0%
Change	52	13.4%	79	20.4%	256	66.1%	387	100.0%
Overall Average	847	18.6%	964	24.0%	2314	57.4%	4128	100.0%

In Table 4.4 above the overall responses for Leadership and Governance dimension shows 56.10% a positive attitude or favorable (34.9% of respondents agree and 21.2% of respondents strongly agree), 19.40% a negative attitude or unfavorable (7.5% of respondents strongly disagree and 11.9% of respondents disagree). Responses for Security Management and Organization dimension shows 54.30% a positive attitude or favorable (31% of respondents agree and 23.3% of respondents strongly agree), 18.90% a negative attitude or unfavorable (7.5% of respondents strongly disagree and 11.4% of respondents disagree). Responses for Security Program Management dimension shows 62.30% a positive attitude or favorable (34.13% of respondents agree and 28.13% of respondents strongly agree), 12.90% a negative attitude or unfavorable (5.17% of respondents strongly disagree and 7.77% of respondents disagree). Responses for User Security Management shows 56.7% a positive attitude or favorable (35.53% of respondents agree and 21.22% of respondents strongly agree), 23.6% a negative attitude or unfavorable (12.77% strongly disagree and 1087% disagree). Responses for Technology Protection shows 48.7% a positive attitude or favorable (32.6% of respondents agree and 6.2% of respondents strongly agree), 23.5% a negative attitude or unfavorable (13.2% of respondents strongly disagree and 15.5% of respondents disagree). The last overall responses for Change shows 66.1% a positive attitude or favorable (39% of respondents agree and 27.1% of respondents strongly agree), 13.4% a negative attitude or unfavorable (7.5% of respondents strongly disagree and 5.9% of respondents disagree).

Leadership and Governance Dimension

Employees of the bank were asked their perception on Leadership and Governance practice in their bank and the result is summarized as shown in figure 4.2 below. Figure 4.2 below shows that graphical representation (bar chart) of the respondents who select "Favorable" with their percentage figures.

Favorable Percent

Statement	Favorable %
The protection of information is perceived as a top priority plan by senior management of the bank.	58.91
Senior managements of the bank are committed to the protection of information assets.	56.59
I believe the bank's information security strategy supports the achievement of its business objectives.	68.99
I believe the risk management process of the bank are adequate.	44.96
Management provides me with guidance to implement the regulatory requirements.	51.16

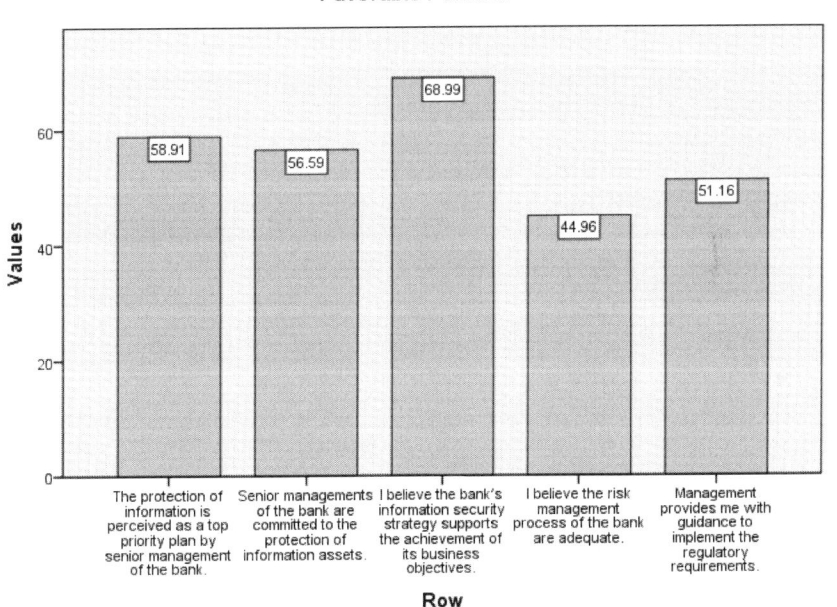

Figure 4.2 summary findings of leadership and governance dimension

As shown in figure 4.2, the finding from the survey shows that 68.99% employees of the surveyed banks shows a positive attitude or most favorable on the statement "I believe the bank's information security strategy supports the achievement of its business objectives". However 44.96% employees of the surveyed banks shows a least favorable on the statement "I believe the risk management process of the bank are adequate".

Inference

Most of the employees of surveyed banks shows a positive attitude or most favorable on most of the statements of the Leadership and Governance dimension. This indicate that surveyed banks are good in leadership and governance. However the surveyed banks are weak in risk management process.

Security Management and Organization Dimension

Employees of the bank were asked their perception on Security Management and Organization practice in their bank and the result is summarized as shown in figure 4.3 below. Figure 4.3 below shows that graphical representation (bar chart) of the respondents who select "Favorable" with their percentage figures.

Favorable Percent

Bar chart values:
- I believe it is necessary to commit time, people, and money to protect information: 81.40
- There are adequate information security specialists/coordinators throughout the bank to ensure the implementation of information security controls: 36.43
- I believe the information security team adequately assist in the implementation of information security control to protect information asset of the bank: 44.96

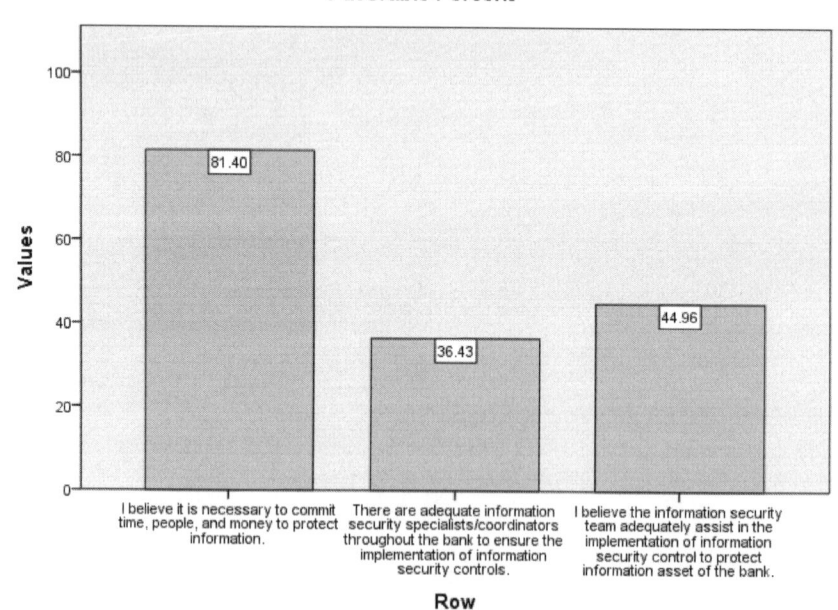

Figure 4.3 summary findings of security management and organization dimension

As shown in the figure 4.3, the finding from the surveyed bank shows that 81.4% employees of the surveyed banks shows a positive attitude or most favorable on the statement "I believe it is necessary to commit time, people, and money to protect information". However 36.43% employees of the surveyed banks shows a least favorable on the statement "There are adequate information security specialist/coordinators throughout the bank to ensure the implementation of information security control".

Inference

Most of the employees of surveyed banks shows a least favorable perception on most of the statements of the Security Management and Organization dimension. This indicate that surveyed banks are weak in security management and organization of the information security team or division even if they are good in accepting the notion of the necessity of committing time, people and money for protecting information and asset of the bank.

Security Program Management Dimension

Employees of the bank were asked their perception on Security Program Management practice in their bank and the result is summarized as shown in figure 4.4 below. Figure 4.4 below shows that graphical representation (bar chart) of the respondents who select "Favorable" with their percentage figures. As shown in the figure 4.4, the finding from the surveyed bank shows that

Favorable Percent

Bar chart values:
- I believe employees should be monitored on their compliance to information security policies and procedures such as measuring the use of e-mail, monitoring which site visited and what software is installed on the computers: **61.24**
- Action should be taken against anyone who does not adhere to the information security policy (e.g. if they share passwords, give out confidential information or visit prohibited internet sites): **59.69**
- I should be seized accountable for my action if I do not adhere to information security policy: **65.89**

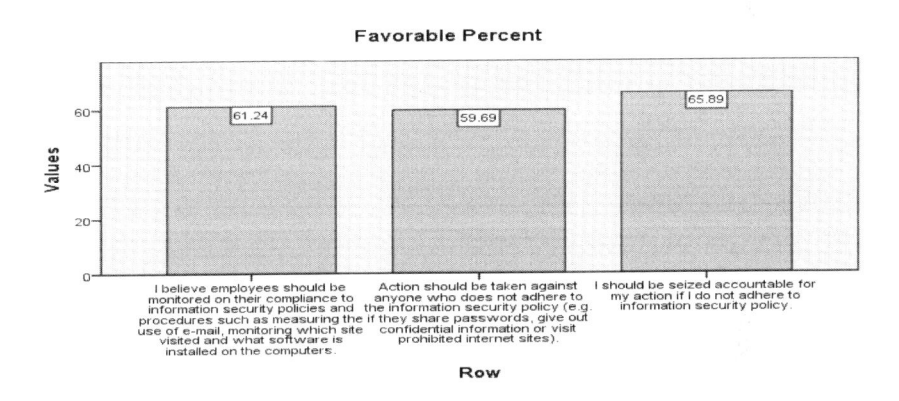

Figure 4.4 summary findings of security program management dimension

65.89% employees of the surveyed banks shows a positive attitude or most favorable on the statement "I should be seized accountable for my action if I do not adhere to information security policy", 61.24% employees of the surveyed banks shows a positive attitude or most favorable on the statement "I believe employees should be monitored on their compliance to information security policies and procedures such as measuring the use e-mail, monitoring which site visited and what software is installed on the computers", 59.69% employees of the surveyed banks shows a positive or most favorable on the statement "Action should be taken against anyone who does not adhere to the information security policy (e.g. if they share their passwords, give out confidential information or visit prohibited internet sites)".

Inference

Most of the employees of surveyed banks shows a positive attitude or most favorable on all of the statements of the Security Program Management dimension. This indicate that surveyed banks are good in security program management.

User Security Management Dimension

Employees of the bank were asked their perception on User Security Management practice in their bank and the result is summarized as shown in figure 4.5 below. Figure 4.5 below shows that graphical representation (bar chart) of the respondents who select "Favorable" with their percentage figures.

Favorable Percent

Figure 4.5 summary finings of user security management dimension

As shown in the figure 4.5, the finding from the surveyed bank shows that 82.17% employees of the surveyed banks shows a positive attitude or most favorable on the statement "I believe there is a need for additional training to use information security controls in order to protect information" and 75.97% employees of the surveyed banks shows a positive attitude or most favorable on the statement "I am aware of information security aspects relating to my job". However 33.33% employees of the surveyed banks shows a least favorable on the statement "I believe that sharing of password should be used to make access to information easier" and 36.43% employees of the surveyed banks shows a least favorable on the statement "I received adequate training to use the applications I require for my daily duties".

Inference

Most of the employees of surveyed banks show a need of adequate training to use the applications they require for their daily duties even if they are aware of information systems security aspects relating to their jobs. And also there is a communication gap between the management and the employees of the surveyed banks on relevant information systems security requirements.

Technology Protection and operation Dimension

Employees of the bank were asked their perception on Technology Protection practice and its operation in their bank and the result is summarized as shown in figure 4.6 below. Figure 4.6 below shows that graphical representation (bar chart) of the respondents who select "Favorable" with their percentage figures.

Favorable Percent

Row	Favorable %
I believe that the information I work with is protected adequately.	54.26
I believe that the information security controls (e.g. passwords) of the applications I use in my daily duties are adequate.	64.34
The protection of information is predominantly the responsibility of the IT/IS business unit.	50.39
I believe the incident management process of the bank is effective in resolving information security incidents	42.64
I believe the building I work in is safeguarded adequately to protect information assets.	48.06
I believe the bank will be able to continue its operation if there is a disaste	42.64
I know what to do in the event of disaster resulting in the loss of computer system, people, and/or premises.	38.76

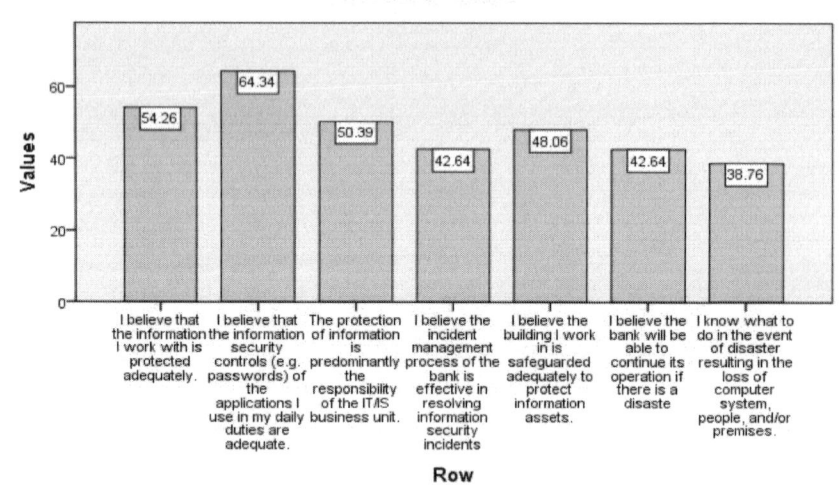

Figure 4.6 summary findings of technology protection and operation dimension

As shown in the figure 4.6, the finding from the surveyed bank shows that 64.34% employees of the surveyed banks shows a positive attitude or most favorable on the statement "I believe that the information security controls (e.g. passwords) of the applications I use in my daily duties are adequate". However 38.76% employees of the surveyed banks shows a least favorable on the statement "I know what to do in the event of disaster resulting in the loss of computer system, people, and/or premises".

Inference

Most of the employees of surveyed banks have little knowledge on the physical security of the banks information and also they have little knowledge on the incident management in resolving information systems security incidents. In addition most of the employees of the surveyed banks do not know what to do in the event of disaster and also do not know whether their bank will be able to continue its operation if there is a disaster.

Change Dimension

Employees of the bank were asked their perception on Technology Protection practice in their bank and the result is summarized as shown in figure 4.7 below. Figure 4.7 below shows that graphical representation (bar chart) of the respondents who select "Favorable" with their percentage figures.

Favorable Percent

- I accept that some inconvenience is necessary to secure information assets: 71.32
- I am prepared to change my working practice in order to ensure the protection of the information assets: 62.02
- Changes in our bank to secure information are accepted positively: 65.12

Figure 4.7 summary findings of change dimension

As shown in the figure 4.7, the finding from the surveyed bank shows that 71.32% employees of the surveyed banks shows a positive attitude or most favorable on the statement "I accept that some inconvenience is necessary to secure information assets", 65.12% employees of the surveyed banks shows a positive attitude or most favorable on the statement "Changes in our bank to secure information are accepted positively" and 62.02% employees of the surveyed banks shows a positive attitude or most favorable on the statement "I am prepared to change my working practice in order to ensure the protection of the information assets".

Inference

Most of the employees of surveyed banks have a positive attitude or favorable on Change dimension. This indicates that changes in their banks to secure information is accepted positively. They are prepared to change their working practice in order to ensure the protection of the information assets.

Each of the IS security culture statements were further investigated to identify the 10 highest (most favorable) and 10 lowest (least favorable) statements. The ten highest statements could be leveraged on to aid with action plans. The 10 lowest statements are identified as a starting point to address the most critical area first. These statements are addressed to improve employee perceptions and IS security culture in the banks of Ethiopia.

The ten highest-ranked statements for the overall result, based on the percentage figures are:
1. I believe there is a need for additional training to use information security controls in order to protect information (82.17%).
2. I believe it is necessary to commit time, people, and money to protect information (81.4%).
3. I am aware of the information aspects relating to my job (75.97%).
4. I think it is important to regard the work I do as part of the intellectual property of the bank (75.19%).
5. I accept responsibility towards the protection of information assets I use for my job (72.87%).
6. I accept that some inconvenience is necessary to secure information assets (71.32%).
7. I believe the bank's information security strategy supports the achievement of its business objectives (68.99%).
8. I should be seized accountable for my action if I do not adhere to information security policy (65.89%).
9. Changes in our bank to secure information are accepted positively (65.12%).
10. I believe that the information security controls (e.g. passwords) of the applications I use in my daily duties are adequate (64.34%).

The ten lowest-ranked statements for the overall results based on the percentage figure are:
1. I believe that sharing password should be used to make access to information easier (33.33%).
2. I received adequate training to use the applications I require for my daily duties (36.43%).
3. There are adequate information security specialists/coordinators throughout the bank to ensure the implementation of information security control (36.43%).
4. I know what to do in the event of disaster resulting in the loss of computer system, people, and/or premises (38.76%).

5. I have adequate knowledge about emergency procedures if I have difficulty on operating the system (40.31%).
6. I believe that management communicates relevant information security requirements to me (40.31%).
7. I believe the incident management process of the bank is effective in resolving information security incidents (42.64%).
8. I believe the bank will be able to continue its operation if there is a disaster resulting in the loss of computer system, people, and/or premises (42.64%).
9. I believe the information security team adequately assist in the implementation of information security control to protect asset of the bank (44.96%).
10. I believe the risk management process of the bank are adequate to identify risks such as the threats of viruses, hackers that could negatively impact on the information of the bank (44.96%).

Comments from Respondent

Comments are obtained from an open paragraph question at the end of the questionnaire. Some comments and suggestions from employees of the surveyed banks are listed below.

- Giving Information System security training for all staffs in bank is important.
- Security policy must be developed based on formal risk assessment result.
- Installing genuine antivirus on all computers of the bank can protect the bank's data.
- Provide IS security awareness should incorporate about password management.

Table 4.5 below provides a summary of the key recommendations. The recommendations are based on the lowest-ranked statements in the overall information security culture report.

Table 4.2 Summary of questionnaire findings and their recommendations for information systems (IS) security culture statements

Statement	Recommendation
I believe that sharing password should be used to make access to information easier (33.33%).	33.33% of employees felt comfortable that sharing password should be to make access to information easier. From the knowledge questions it was evident that most employees understand the risk when they share their passwords to other employees. **Actions:** - There should be an approved policy and procedure in the bank in order to enforce and control all over information systems security activities of the bank. - The awareness plan should incorporate the password and password related activities of the bank.
I received adequate training to use the applications I require for my daily duties (36.43%). I have adequate knowledge about emergency procedures if I have difficulty on operating the system (40.31%).	Only 28.68% of the bank's employees felt comfortable that they received adequate training in information security. 82.17% of the bank's employees therefore indicated that there is a need for additional training and 36.43% of employees felt that they received adequate training to use applications they require for their daily duties. From the knowledge questions it was evident that most employees understand what is meant with information security. **Actions:** - Top management should believe more strongly that there is a need for additional training compared to trainees. This could be as a result of top management understanding of the business risk the bank faces in terms of information security. - Non-technical staffs of the bank were significantly more negative compared to the IT staffs. Therefore a focused training session could be considered for them. - The information security training that will be conducted in the banks of Ethiopia should focus on the practical usage of information security controls.
There are adequate information security specialists/coordinators throughout the bank to ensure the implementation of information security control (36.43%). I believe the information security team adequately assist in the implementation of information security control to protect asset of the bank (44.96%).	Only 36.43% of employees felt comfort that there are adequate information security specialists/coordinators in their banks. But most of the surveyed banks employees felt uncomfortable on the effectiveness of their information security teams/coordinators. **Actions:** - Top management should believe more strongly that there is a need for additional training compared to trainees. This could be as a result of top management understanding of the business risk the bank faces in terms of information security. - Managements should hire qualified/certified information security officer.

	• Managements should facilitate information security related trainings for information security experts of the banks of Ethiopia.
• Managements should conduct a workshop for the staffs of the bank with the involvement of information security teams in order to discuss the key issues and as a result to come up with their deliberate solutions.
I know what to do in the event of disaster resulting in the loss of computer system, people, and/or premises (38.76%).
I believe the bank will be able to continue its operation if there is a disaster resulting in the loss computer system, people, and/or premises (42.64%).	There is/could be a sign-off business continuity plan in place in the banks, but it has not been communicated to employees yet. Therefore there is a communication and awareness problem in the banks.
Actions:
• The awareness plan should incorporate business continuity as one of the key areas to communicate to staffs of the banks. E-mail, web-based training and the intranet can be considered for communication channels for the employees of the bank.
I believe that management communicates relevant information security requirements to me (40.31%).	Only 40.31% of employees felt comfortable that the management communicates relevant information security requirements to them. Therefore there is a communication gap between the employees and the management.
Actions:
• Management should conduct a workshop with employees to understand the reason why employees were negative.
• Management should communicate to users the requirements to manage information security as well as to address the issues brought forward in the workshop and bridge the communication gap.
I believe the incident management process of the bank is effective in resolving information security incidents (42.64%).	Only 42.64% of employees felt comfortable that the incident management process of the banks is effective in resolving information security incidents. Therefore there a problem in the operation of IT department in incident management process.
Actions:
• Management should conduct a workshop with employees to understand the reason why employees were negative.
• Management should communicate with IT department director, IT security managers and other relevant divisions or departments on the incidents management process of the bank in resolving information security incidents.
I believe the risk management process of the bank are adequate to identify risks such as the threats of viruses, hackers that could	Only 44.96% of the employees felt comfortable with the adequacy of the risk management process of the banks. Therefore there is an information systems security governance problem in the banks.
Actions:

Page | 47

negatively impact on the information of the bank (44.96%).	- Management should conduct a workshop with employees to understand the reason why employees were negative. - Top managements and board of directors should communicate and give very big attention to the risk management process of the bank. - Top managements and board of directors should give a direction to managements on how to build and implement adequate risk management process of the bank.

4.5.2 Interview findings

The analysis of qualitative data is done using observer impression. Interview findings are described in terms of words. The aim of this analysis is to examine the different IT security managers' and senior IT security officers view and idea regards to the management of information security in banks the interviewees hold, as well as to arrive at condensed descriptions of these views.

The organization of this section is presented as follows: First, each interview question is presented along with a condensed text that describes each interviewee's view. Then, a final synthesis is made that integrates these views under each question.

Types of standard or framework a surveyed banks have employed or follow
Question 1. Do you have IS security framework in your bank, what kind of standard or framework did your bank follow?

An interviewee from bank 1 clarified that there is no IS security model or baseline implemented in the bank rather there is an unapproved policy and procedure that the bank applied or implemented to safeguard its information assets. In addition there was no common information security standards and frameworks that the bank follow as a best practice. In a similar way two interviewees from bank 1 have also the same comment.

An interviewee from bank 2 explains that there is no IS security model or baseline implemented in the bank rather there is a fragmented policy and procedure that the bank applied or implemented to protect its information assets. In addition there was no common information security standards and frameworks that the bank adopts as a best practice. Two interviewees from bank 2 conform the above interviewees idea, but even if the bank does not have a model or baseline the bank tries to use some known standards as a best practice like ISO/IEC27001&2:2005 standard, PCIDSS in some conditions when it necessary.

An interviewee from bank 3 explains that there is no IS security model or baseline implemented in the bank rather there is a fragmented policy and procedure that the bank applied to protect its information assets. In addition there was no common information security standards and frameworks that the bank adopts as a best practice. Two interviewees from bank 3 also conform the above interviewees idea, but even if the bank does not have a framework the bank tries to use some known standards as a best practice like ISO/IEC27001&2:2005 standard, COBIT, and PCIDSS in some conditions when it necessary.

An interviewee from bank 4 explains that there is no IS security model or baseline implemented in the bank rather there is a fragmented policy and procedure that the bank applied or implemented to protect its information assets. In addition there was no common information security standards and frameworks that the bank adopts as a best practice. Two interviewees from bank 4 also conform the above interviewees idea, but even if the bank does not have a model the bank tries to use some known standards as a best practice like ISO/IEC27001&2:2005 standard, COBIT, and PCIDSS in some conditions when it necessary. At the current situation the bank has decided to start to use PCI DSS as a standard.

An interviewee from bank 5 explained that there is no IS security model or baseline implemented in the bank rather there is an unapproved policy and procedure that the bank applied or implemented to safeguard its information assets. In addition there was no common information security standards and frameworks that the bank follow as a best practice or a standard. In a similar way two interviewees from bank 5 have also the same comment.

Summary of views

All interviewees of the five banks explained that there is no IS security model or baseline implemented in their bank rather there is unapproved policy and procedure implemented in their banks in order to safeguard their banks information assets. In addition there was no common information security standards and frameworks that the surveyed banks follow as a standard or a best practice. However from five banks, three banks tries to use some international wide information security standards as a best practice for their banks in some conditions when it is necessary. The standards the banks use as a best practice are like ISO/IEC27001, COBIT, NIST, ITIL, and PCI DSS etc. Actually one bank is at the initiation point to use PCI DSS as a standard.

Factors that constitute or reflect IS security culture in the surveyed banks

Question 2. What are the factors that constitute or reflect IS security culture in your bank?

All interviewees from bank 1 agrees on the idea of "a well formed information systems security policy and procedure that is approved by top management of the bank can strongly constitute IS security culture in the bank". Similarly all interviewees from bank 2, 3 and 4 also share the ideas of the interviewees from bank 1. However all the interviewees perception from bank 5 on the establishment of IS security culture in the bank is "a well formed IT/IS security charter of IT security office which is approved by the top management of the bank can create IS security culture in the bank".

Summary of views

All interviewees of the five surveyed banks clarified that in order to establish IS security culture in the bank, there should be an approved IS security policy and procedure and IT/IS security charter for IT security office.

Factors that have direct influence (positively or negatively) on IS security culture in surveyed banks

Question 3. What are the factors that have direct influence on IS security culture in your bank?

All interviewees from bank 1 tried to mention activities like: lack of top management support, lack of skilled information security staffs, NBE (National Bank of Ethiopia) rules and regulations, lack of awareness on IS security for the top management and employees of the bank, happening of unwanted security incidents made by employees (intentionally or unintentionally), top management support and involvement in the IS security aspect and organizational structure of information security office were the factors that have a direct influence on IS security culture of their banks. Especially the organizational structure of the information security office have an impact (positive or negative) on the overall activities of IS security culture of the bank.

All interviewees from bank 2 mentioned that activities such as: lack of top management support, conducting a focused-based awareness and training for the employees of the bank, organizational structure of information security office, lack of budget for information security office, lack of information security staffs and the new establishment of combining/centralizing the banks network were the factors that have direct influence on IS security culture of their bank.

All interviewees from bank 3 explained that events like: lack of top management support, lack of awareness of the employees of the bank, organizational structure of information security office, lack of information security automated tools, individual behavior can influence information security culture of the bank and negligence problem were the factors that have direct influence on IS security culture of their bank.

All interviewees from bank 4 mentioned that activities such as: top management involvement, conducting a case-based awareness for the top management about information security breaches and incidents, lack of awareness of top management about IS security, organizational structure of information security office, Knowledge gap between the top management and employees with information security office and its operation, absence information security automated tools and lack of adequate training for information security staffs were the factors that have direct influence on IS security culture of their bank.

All interviewees from bank 5 mentioned events like: lack of top management support, lack of awareness on IS security and its operation for the employees of the bank, organizational structure of information security office, lack of adequate training for information security staffs, lack of budget for information security office, unavailability of institutions that give IS security training, currently available staffs do not sufficiently understand the banking business and its risks, lack of IS security governance, lack of board of directors and top management commitment and absence of IS security framework in the country were the factors that have a direct influence on IS security culture of their banks. One interviewee from bank 5 explained that the main factor that have direct and strong influence on the IS security culture in the bank is Information Systems security is relatively new and unexplored domain for Ethiopian country.

Summary of views

All interviewees from the five surveyed banks have the same perception on the absence of IS security model or framework in the banks and countrywide is one of the most significant factor that have direct influence on IS security culture of their banks. Most of the interviewees from the five surveyed banks have also added their perception by stating lack of top management support is also a factor that have direct influence on IS security culture of their banks. An interviewee from bank 1 has explained that lack of awareness throughout the bank have a direct and strong influence on the IS security culture of the bank, similarly three interviewees from another surveyed banks have shared the idea of the above interviewee from bank 1. Another interviewee from bank 3 explains that NBE (National Bank of Ethiopia) rules and regulations are also have direct influence on the IS security culture of the banks of Ethiopia, similarly another interviewees from bank 4 and 5 also confirmed the idea of an interviewee from bank 3. An interviewee from bank 2 clarifies that knowledge gap between the top management and employees of the bank with information security office and its operation have direct influence on IS security culture of the bank, likewise another interviewee from bank 2 also share the idea of the above interviewee from bank 2. Most of the interviewees from five surveyed banks states that organizational structure of information security office have a direct influence on the IS security culture of their banks. Lack of skilled information security staffs, lack of information security automated tools, individual behavior, Absence information security automated tools, lack of adequate training for information security staffs, lack of budget given for information security office, unavailability of institutions that give IS security training, currently available staffs do not sufficiently understand the banking business and its risks, and lack of IS security governance were factors that have direct influence on the IS security culture of the banks which is mentioned by most of the interviewees of the five surveyed bank.

Main barriers to address the lack of IS security awareness's in the surveyed banks
Question 4. What are the main barriers to address the lack of IS security awareness's?

All interviewees from bank 1, 2 and 3 have also similar explanation on the barriers to address the lack of IS security awareness such as lack of budget given to information security office, lack of skilled information security staffs, lack of information security tools and lack of information security staffs commitment. In addition to the above barriers an interviewee from bank 2 explains that the commitment of information security staffs to conduct an awareness throughout the bank is weak due to lack of information security tools, salary of the staffs, absence of incentives in order to appreciate the staff's work, absence of appreciation letter given by the middle management of the bank and uncomfortable working are in the bank.

All interviewees from bank 4 and 5 have also similar explanation is that one of the most barriers to address the lack of IS security awareness is lack of top management and board of directors buy in. Two interviewees from bank 4 and one interviewee from bank 5 similarly explain in detail that when top management and board of directors of the banks don't understand and don't have enough awareness about the security aspect of the bank, they cannot give a very big attention on IS security activities and its operation. As a result the top management and board of directors cannot allocate sufficient budget for the information security office and also they cannot assign comparable information security staffs for the information security office. Therefore "lack of lack of top management and board of directors buy in" is the main barrier to address the lack of IS security awareness's which is explained by the interviewees of bank 4 and 5.

Summary of views

All interviews of the five banks mentioned the main barriers to address the lack of IS security awareness's such as lack of budget given to information security office, lack of skilled information security staffs, lack of information security tools and lack of information security staffs commitment. Lack of information security staffs is one of the most barriers to conduct IS security awareness effectively and sufficiently for the employee of the banks. The main reason is there are very few information security staffs hired by the surveyed banks. The other but most importantly obstacle to conduct IS security awareness throughout the bank is lack of top management and board of directors buy in.

Improvement of security compliance in the surveyed banks
Question 5. How can you improve security compliance in your bank?

All interviewees of the five banks (**Bank 1-5)** have also similar clarification on how to improve security compliance, what they states is the key point to improve security compliance in the bank is implementing an approved IS security policy and procedure in the bank in order to enforce and control information security aspects of the banks and collaboration work with IT audit divisions and IT departments can be easily improve IS security compliance in the banks. One of the interviewee from bank 3 explains in detail is that when there is an approved IS security policy and procedures implemented in the bank, IT auditors will evaluate and control whether the overall IT related activities and operations related to security are comply with the banks policy and procedure.

Summary of views

All interviewees of the five surveyed banks have explained that in order to improve security compliance in the bank an approved IS security policy and procedure must be implemented and there must be a strong collaboration work with IT audit division, IT security office/division and IT/IS department.

Summary of interview findings

The results, from the summary below specify how the interviewee's (senior IT security officers, IT security managers and IT/IS directors) perceive IS security practices in their banks. The intention of this research is to arrive at an accommodation of their view, perception and activities rather than trying to emphasize the differences among them.

All interviewees of the five banks explained that there is no IS security model or baseline in their bank.
- All interviewees of the five banks clarified that in order to establish IS security culture in the bank, there should be an approved IS security charter, policy and procedure.
- The main factors that have negative influence on the IS security culture of the banks which are explained by the interviewees are listed below:
  - Lack of top management support and commitment
  - Lack of skilled information security officers
  - Lack of employees awareness and Lack of budget
  - Absence of IS security framework in the bank
  - Lack of information security tools
- Main success factors which are explained by the interviewees are:
  - Top management involvement and support
  - Empowering information security office
  - Conducting continuous training for employees
  - Awareness throughout the bank
  - Bridging the communication gap between the information security office with top management and employees of the bank
- All interviews of the five banks mentioned the main barriers to address the lack of IS security awareness's such as:
  - Lack of budget given to information security office
  - Lack of skilled information security staffs
  - Lack of information security staffs commitment
- All employees of the five banks clarified that implementing an approved IS security policy and procedure will strongly improve security compliance in the bank.

The literature review, questionnaire and interview findings, and the researchers own experience shows that there is no local Information Systems (IS) security framework: that will help as a guideline in developing and implementing IS security policy to secure data in the banking industry of Ethiopia.

Questionnaire and interview findings show that there is a lack of IS security awareness in the banking industry in Ethiopia. Similarly a work in [8] stated that 'Information security awareness in the banking sector in Ethiopia is unsatisfactory. Consequently, the level of proper information security governance in the banking sector in Ethiopia is a critical area of improvement'. In addition to the above mentioned finding, another interview finding from this research survey show that there is a lack of IS security governance in the banking industry in Ethiopia. Similarly authors in [30] attempt to confirm that the recent incidents of information security governance failure such as those at Baring, Enron and Ameriquest banks emphasize the need for revisiting the current information systems security governance practice and adopt more strict means to ensure security. In support of one of the practical problems faced in Ethiopian banking industry, Tubin in his work [43] says the most common threat or risk to banking and financial institution is phishing attack.

4.6 Summary

The research findings of the survey (questionnaire) and its interpretations were presented under each question items whereas inferences are stated at the end of each security dimension. The aim of the field study is to discover the state of the information system security practice of banks involved in financial services to the people using IT. Questionnaires and interview questions were used as instrument to carry out the study. The questionnaires were used to collect data about IS security culture and knowledge of employees on IS security area and the student researcher own additional points which are relevant to inspect IS security culture and knowledge of employees on IS security practice in the banking industry.

This study research findings were classified into two major areas such as; findings from the interviews and findings from questionnaires. Questionnaire findings provided insight into the knowledge of employees on IS security area and how IS security culture is practiced in the surveyed banks. Findings from Interview clarified the general issues in information security in addition to supplement the questionnaires. The survey was carried out in 5 Ethiopian banks from November 05 - 25, 2016. The survey was done in person to increase the response rate and also succeed in the study even though it is time taking to get responses from a given bank.

Questionnaire results from data analysis were presented that address the main components of Information Security Culture Framework (ISCF) which make up the themes .The data analysis result is depicted using charts in percentage which refers to the number of banks having or not having certain IS security culture and employees knowledge on IS security areas. The knowledge questions were analysed separately from the culture questions, as these two sets of questions each had different objectives. The knowledge questions are used to provide background in analysing the culture questions and they focus what employees "know". The IS security culture questions are used to measure the level of IS security culture in the bank and focus on the opinion and perception of employees regarding the information security components defined in the Information Security Culture Framework (ISCF). All the statements are categorized in to six dimensions based on the ISCF except the remaining one dimension of ISCF, the reason why one dimension which is "information security policy" is left is that from preliminary assessment it was believed that in the surveyed banks of Ethiopia implementing IS security policy in the bank is almost none or informal and not known by the staff, as a result in this research it was taken as a weakness or finding of this research. The six components ISCF were Leadership and governance dimension, Security management and organization dimension, security program management dimension, User security management dimension, Technology protection and operation dimension, and Change dimension. Each of the IS security culture statements were further investigated to identify the 10 highest (most favorable) and 10 lowest (least favorable) statements. The ten highest statements could be leveraged on to aid with action plans. The 10 lowest statements are identified as a starting point to address the most critical area first. These statements are addressed to improve employee perceptions and IS security culture in the banks of Ethiopia.

The analysis of qualitative data is done using observer impression. Interview findings are described in terms of words. The aim of this analysis is to examine the different IT directors, IT managers, IT security managers' and senior IT security officers view and idea regards to the issues and practices of information security in banks the interviewees hold, as well as to arrive at condensed descriptions of these views. The organization of the interview section were structured in the form like: First, each interview question were presented along with a condensed text that describes each interviewee's view. Then, a final synthesis is made that integrates these views under each interview question.

The finding of the interview data were summarized along with the questionnaire findings in a way suitable to be managed for further analysis. The author of this research being as a facilitator, conduct a discussion with the IT security managers of the surveyed banks to draw a rich picture by using a Soft Systems approach.

CHAPTER FIVE
DESIGN OF THE FRAMEWORK USING SSM

5.1 Overview

This chapter discusses the rationale for using the approach (Soft Systems Methodology), apply SSM in its seven-stages in order to explore the IS security problems and issues that are facing in Ethiopian banking industry using rich picture with the combination of summary of the surveys (questionnaire and interview findings) and develop an IS security framework for Ethiopian banking industry. After developing the conceptual model the author compare the model with the expressed problem situation in order to achieve possible changes suggested by key participants of the SSM group identify and define desirable and feasible changes to improve the problem situation.

5.2 Why do we adopt SSM

Checkland's SSM methodology was used to analysed IS security related problems because it was seen to have the potential to allow an in depth investigation of the human dimension of the problem. Numerous reasons lead us to use SSM such as: As defined by Checkland SSM is not a system development methodology rather it is a methodology to identify changes and also it is a human problem and process oriented not technique oriented. A number of models can be built to represent different viewpoints of different stakeholders and exploration of problem situations are used to decide an action for desirable changes, SSM allowed us to use appropriately establish the current position on IS security related problems and issues from the stakeholders perspectives, SSM emphasis on the process of inquiry as a system is an intuitive alternative to the hard systems tradition of taking a systematic view of the world [Jenkins 1969, Checkland 1999], SSM provides a technique for analysing the qualitative aspect of IS security and management problems, SSM has been developed for use in ill-structured or messy problem contexts such as those discovered during this study, SSM in action prevents decision makers from rushing into poorly thought-out solutions based on preconceived ideas about an assumed problem, SSM is useful in exploring problems by providing a structured approach for examining the views and concerns of stakeholders, and SSM is flexible and has been adopted in different fields [44, 45, 46, 47, 48, 49, 50].

5.3 Rich picture and summary of the survey

In this study the author of this research apply SSM in its seven-stages in order to explore the IS security problems and issues that are facing in Ethiopian banking industry using rich picture with the combination of summary of the surveys (questionnaire and interview findings) to develop an IS security framework for Ethiopian banking industry.

5.3.1 Summary of the survey (questionnaire and interview findings)
The results obtained from the survey such as questionnaire and interview findings summary are described below.

Summary of questionnaire findings

The results obtained from questionnaire shows that the surveyed banks of Ethiopia are weak in risk management process of IS security activities, which indicates that the risk management processes of the banks is not effective in identifying risks such as the threats of viruses, hackers and other IS security related risks that could have negative impact on the information or assets of the banks. On the other hand the result shows that the surveyed banks of Ethiopia are weak in security management and organization of information security team or division which shows that there is a lack of sufficient information security specialists or coordinators to assist and ensure the implementation of IS security controls effectively to protect the assets of their banks. Questionnaire results also show that employees of the surveyed banks have lack of knowledge about emergency procedures when the have difficulty on operating the system (automated system), as a consequence most of the surveyed banks employees show a need of adequate IS security training to use the application they require for their daily duties. Another questionnaire result shows that the incident management process of the surveyed banks of Ethiopia is not effective in resolving IS security incidents, as a result most of the surveyed banks employees have little knowledge on the incident management process of their banks in resolving IS security incidents. In addition to the above questionnaire result another questionnaire outcome shows that there is a communication gap between the management and employees of the surveyed banks on relevant IS security requirements, because of that most of the employees of the surveyed banks do not know how to do in the event of disaster and do not know whether their bank will be able to continue its operation if there is a disaster resulting in the loss of computer system, people and premises. At last a result that shows most of the employees of the surveyed banks have little knowledge on the physical security of their banks information, which purely indicates that there is a lack of IS security awareness throughout the banks of Ethiopia.

Summary of interview findings

The results obtained from the interview has shown that there is no IS security framework in Ethiopian banking industry and also in the country. Interviewees have also explained that implementing an approved IS security policy will establish a commonly held IS security culture and will strongly improve security compliance in the banks of Ethiopia. Lack of budget given to information security office, lack of skilled information security staffs, lack of information security staffs commitment were also the main obstacles to address IS security awareness throughout the banks of Ethiopia. Lack of top management support and commitment, lack of skilled information security officers, lack of employee's awareness, lack of budget, lack of information security tools and absence of IS security framework in the bank were the key leading factors that have negative influence on the IS security culture of the banks of Ethiopia. On the contrast top management involvement and support, empowering information security office, conducting continuous training for employees and awareness about IS security throughout the bank are the main success factors for implementing IS security culture for the banking industry in Ethiopia.

5.3.2 Rich picture
Understanding the problem situation: stage 1 and 2

During the first two stages of the methodology (SSM) the problem situation is understood then expressed. In the initial stage there is no clear definition of the problem situation rather it needs to be examined and understood by the involved stakeholders. In stage two, the problem situation is expressed, preferably using a "rich picture" where the system thinker develops a detail description of the problem. Many different views were investigated. A rich picture diagram aims to highlight the primary purpose of the organization at high levels and to identify the issues which matter or area of concern in the development of effective information systems security. The drawing of a rich picture establishes the interconnections and relationships that exist between various components and stakeholders in the research context [44, 51]. Data for the rich picture were obtained from interview with stakeholders at each site, literature review, and questionnaires. In this stage we don't completely define the problem rather we clarify the problem solving and problem content system and link them together.

In this research, the author of this research has professional knowledge of information systems security. As a result the author occupied the role of problem solver. The author of this research can call on other resources such as the combined experience of the participants, evidence from the surveys. The role of the problem solver is to explain the problem content system and then apply SSM to take action to solve the problem or to explain it again on behalf of the problem owner. Top management and Board of Directors, IT staffs, IT Audit staffs, IT security staffs, and Non-technical staffs of the surveyed Ethiopian of banks occupied the role of problem owner. According to [26, 52] the client is someone who wants to do something and commission the study. In this research client do not exist in this sense but exists in a diffusion form, not as a single person or organization. These partial clients are the author, IT professionals, IT Audit experts, and IT security experts and IT security managers of Ethiopian banks.

To understand and express the problem situation the author of this research conduct an un-structured interviews for discussion with 5 IT Security Managers of the five surveyed bank of Ethiopia. The selection process was done by selecting one IT Security Manager from each five surveyed banks of Ethiopia. Through the discussion the author was able to identify organizational activities, relationships which as a whole constitute the problem situation. In drawing a rich picture there is no universal set of symbols to apply, as a result the author of this research try to draw by his own. In this research, there are 5 actors such as: Top management bodies, IT staffs, IT Audit staffs, IT security staffs and Organizational staffs (Non-Technical staffs). All these actors are considered problem owners. External parties were also represented in the figure shown below. The keys for the rich pictures are:

| External party | Thinking bubbles | Conflicts | Human aspect (Actors) |

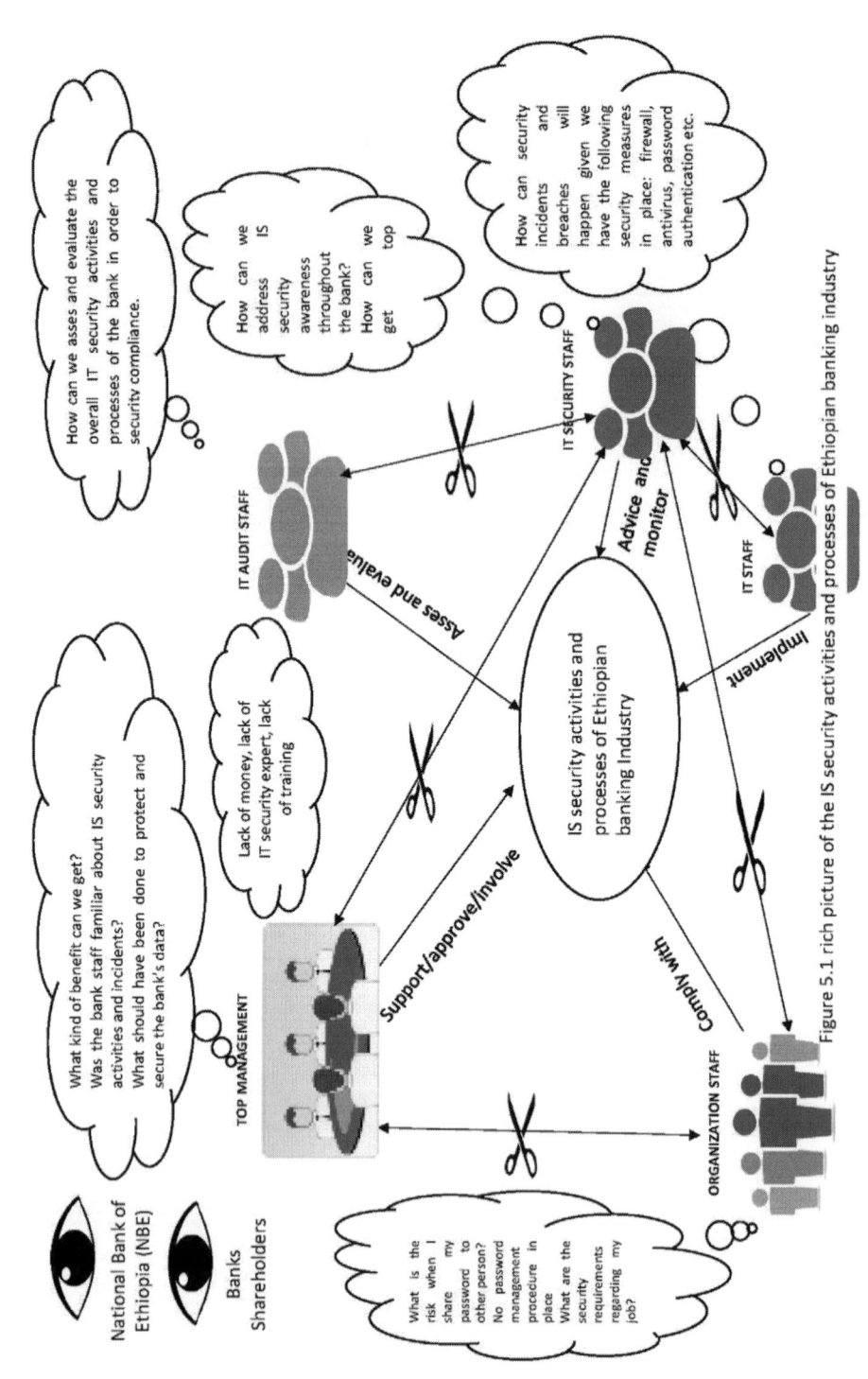

Figure 5.1 rich picture of the IS security activities and processes of Ethiopian banking industry

In the rich picture diagram human figure represents the key actors in the system. Obstacles, issues of concern, expectation of actors are represented as think bubbles, conflicts between actors are represented by crossed swords and external parties are represented by an eye.

5.4 Root Definition of relevant system and Conceptual model

In this section two stages of SSM will be described in detail that is defining the relevant system (stage 3 of SSM) and developing conceptual model (stage 4 of SSM). In defining a relevant systems the author of this research combine and accommodate 5 IT security Managers impression with his own professional skill, literature review, questionnaire findings, interview findings and rich picture in order to define relevant systems for the complex problem situation.

Root Definition of relevant system: stage 3

In this stage developing a root definition of relevant system is taken place, the author of this research identify human activity system relevant to the complex problem situation and develop a root definitions of the relevant systems from the rich picture and findings of the survey. Developing the root definition is a fundamental activity in the SSM methodology where a human activity system relevant to the complex problem situation is identified and defined. As defined by [53] a root definition is a short verbal statement of the relevant system. The root definition should include a structured description of the elements captured in the defined system with a clear statement of the activities it should perform.

The main notion of the root definition is to capture the basic elements involved in the system. There are two different types of systems in this stage such as primary task and issue based. The primary task in this research to create a commonly held and shared information systems security culture among the staffs of the bank to transfer information, knowledge, awareness and experience among the staffs in order to protect the data's or assets of Ethiopian banking industries. And also issues and concerns are captured in this research. Examples considered in this research include: social and cultural issues, peoples concern, and organizational issues.

In this research nine human activities for the conceptual model has been identified as follows:
1. Top management support and involvement as part of the relevant system
2. Organizational structure as part of the relevant system
3. IT/IS security steering committee as part of the relevant system
4. Communication as part of the relevant system
5. Education and training as part of the relevant system
6. Awareness as part of the relevant system
7. IS security policy and maintenance as part of the relevant system
8. Collaboration work as part of the relevant system
9. IS security ownership as part of the relevant system

According to [26], root definition should be tested against a group of elements known by the mnemonic "CATWOE" derive from Customer, Actors, Transformation, Weltanschauung worldview, Owners, Environment.

The selected 5 IT security Managers from each surveyed banks of Ethiopia try to define and come up with their own root definition by their own perception. After that the author of this research (problem solver) conduct a discussion to combine and integrate the 5 IT security managers idea in to an accommodation of their idea to produce an accepted root definition of the system.

The general layout of an accepted root definition IS security system is:

> "Ethiopian banks owned Information Systems security system to create a commonly held and shared information systems security culture within the bank and to protect the physical and information technology assets of the bank by involving top management in information systems security activities, by establishing IT/IS security steering committee, by implementing IS security awareness throughout the bank, by supplying adequate training for the IT security experts, by establishing a strong and consistent collaboration work between business units, by empowering IT security office, by establishing and implementing IS security policy in the bank, by creating an effective communication channel and mechanism, and by creating security ownership among all staffs of the bank in order to ensure the confidentiality, availability and integrity of the bank's assets and information."

The "CATWOE" elements of the root definition are illustrated along a brief description of each of the mnemonic elements listed below:

C: Customers of the system are those who are either beneficiaries or victims of the system activities. Therefore all staffs of Ethiopian banks are the victims while top management and board of directors, IT security experts are the main beneficiaries.

A: Actors of the system are those who actually carry out the main activities of the system and transforms its input to outputs. The researcher, all staffs of Ethiopian banks including the 5 IT security managers are the main actors of the defined system.

T: The transformation process carried out by the system. What does the system do in order to transform inputs to outputs. The need to create a common IS security framework and apply into the banking industry in Ethiopia.

W: The weltanschauung or viewpoint that makes the root definition meaningful. In this research the weltanschauung that makes the root definition meaningful is the need to create a commonly held and shared IS security culture within the bank in order to assure the confidentiality, availability and integrity of the bank's data or asset.

O: The system owner is the one who has the ultimate power over the system and can stop it. The CEO (Chief Executive Officer) or president of the bank and Board of directors are the main owner of the system.

E: The environmental constraints the system will operate within. NBE (National Bank of Ethiopia) rules and regulations, budget constraint, Ethiopian people's IS security awareness level culture, ethical conduct of staff's behavior, shareholders of the bank are the main environmental constraints in this system.

The performance of the system can measured by the 3E's which is:

E: Efficacy, the system will create a security culture within the bank to protect the physical and information technology assets of the bank.

E: Efficiency, the system can be implemented and practiced in Ethiopian banks with the existing resources and the minimum resources.

E: Effectiveness, the system will create a security culture among all staffs of the bank in order to assure and maintain a secure environment that supports the mission and vision of the bank.

Developing a Conceptual model: stage 4

This stage builds a conceptual model based on the root definitions. The model building phase starts from the root definition and asks what activities would have to take place in system in order to meet the requirement of the root definition.

Checkland in [26] claimed that this stage is a logical model of the activities and processes that must be carried out in order to satisfy the root definition produced in stage two. In addition of the above Checkland's request logical model of the activities and processes that must be carried out in order to satisfy the root definition are also produced from interview and questionnaire findings of this research empirical study.

The author of this research utilizes a "rich picture" created in stage two of the Soft Systems Methodology (SSM) and findings of the survey (interview and questionnaire) as a primary source for developing a conceptual model of the activities and processes of the system that must be carried out in order to satisfy the root definitions produced in stage three of the approach (SSM).

In this research investigating the problems suggested by the rich picture and findings of the survey leads to the following conceptual models which define how activities should proceed for the system to function properly and effectively. In this research 9 logical model of the activities and processes that must be carried out in order to satisfy the root definitions that are relevant to the system are defined and describe in detail below.

1. Top management support and involvement theme

In order to assure the confidentiality, availability and integrity of information throughout the banking industry top management support and involvement plays a critical role in assuring and controlling whether the IS security processes and activities are aligned with the strategic goals of the bank. Therefore a strong, consistent support and involvement of top management is needed for creating a commonly held and shared IS security culture and for securing overall data and information's of the bank of Ethiopia.

The main requirements of top management support and involvement theme can be defined as follows:
- Place IS security on the board's agenda.
- Identify and assign IT/IS security leaders, hold them accountable and ensure support for them.
- Assign IS security to a key committee and ensure adequate support for them.
- Define and allocate responsibilities for IS security risk management process and activities of the bank, particularly for acceptance residual risks.
- Approve new or existing IS security policy of the bank.

2. Organizational structure theme

Organizational structure defines how activities such as task allocation, coordination and supervision are directed toward the achievement of organizational aim. IT security office or division should have an appropriate power in order to implement and control IS security activities and processes of the banks. Therefore IT security office or division should be structured in the bank properly and adequately to address and control all the IS security processes and activities of the bank.

The main requirements of the organizational structure theme can be defined as follows:
- Develop or restructuring the IT security office or division independent of IT department and the CIO or the vice president of IT. Structure the IT security office to report directly to the CEO (Chief Executive Officer) or president of the bank. Develop or restructure the organizational structure of the bank by allocating the IT security office to report directly to the CEO (Chief Executive Officer) or the president of the bank in order to advocate IT/IS security as a business enabler and to have sufficient level of authority that enable them to adequately and effectively perform their assigned tasks.
- Empower the IT security office or division with sufficient authority.

3. IT/IS security steering committee theme

Information security affects all aspects of an organisation. To ensure that all stakeholders affected by security considerations are involved, IS/IT security steering committee of executives should be formed in Ethiopian banking industry. Members of such a committee may include, amongst others, the chief executive officer (CEO) or designee, business unit executives, chief financial officer (CFO), Chief Information Officer (CIO)/IT director, chief security officer (CSO)/IT security Manager, Chief Information Security Officer (CISO), human resources, legal, risk management, audit, operations and public relations.

Information systems security steering committee serves as an effective communication channel for management's aims and directions and provides an ongoing basis for ensuring alignment of the security programme with organizational objectives. A book in [54] defines that IS security steering committee is also used as an instrument in achieving behavior change toward a culture that promotes good security practices and policy compliance.

The main requirements of the IT/IS security steering committee theme can be defined as follows:
- Establish IS security steering committee that have actors from the concerned department and executives of the bank that can:
    - Communicate the IS security program to the bank.
    - Communicate the importance of IS security objectives and the need for continual improvement.
    - Communicate IS security breaches and incidents to the bank staffs and to public.
    - Monitor and measure the IS security risk management process of the bank.
    - Define and allocate IS security resources (like budget, tools, people etc.).
    - Coordinate the creation of IS security incident management teams.
    - Implements IS security awareness program.
    - Provides approval of new or modification of IS security policies of the bank.

- To provide and use effective decision making technique

4. Communication theme

Management need to communicate with staffs of the bank about IS security requirements of the application they use for their daily duties of work, IS security policy of the bank needs to be communicated to all staffs of the bank in order to create security ownership among all staffs of the bank and improve security compliance among the staffs. In addition to the above mentioned requirements IT security office needs to communicate with top management and board of directors about the necessary of IS security on the contribution of the objective of the banks strategy.

The main requirements of communication theme can be defined as follows:
- Define information and knowledge that needs to be shared about IS security processes and requirements.
- Define IS security policy that needs to be communicated to the bank staffs.
- Identify staffs application that are needed.
- Identify IS security incidents and breaches that needs to be shared to the public.
- Deliver an effective communication mechanism.

5. Education and training theme

Determined assistances cannot be gained from the bank unless all staffs including IT security staff receive an excellent training and education. Therefore, an adequate training and education program must be provided.
The main requirements of education and training theme can be defined as follows:
- Provide sufficient tools and facilities for IT security experts.
- Supply instruction guidance and manuals that can be easily understood.
- Offer suitable IS security related courses to cover specific topics.
- Provide well trained lecturers.

6. Awareness theme

Maximum protection the bank's data cannot be assured from the staff of the banks unless all staffs including board of directors and executive management obtain an ongoing and continuous IS security awareness. Therefore, an ongoing and continuous IS security awareness program must be established throughout the bank.
The main requirements of awareness theme can be defined as follows:
- Conduct a case-based awareness for top management about IS security incidents and breaches happened in the bank and all over the world.
- Conduct a continuous and an ongoing awareness throughout the bank about IS security activities and processes.
- Conduct a group or focused-based and role-based awareness about IS security activities and processes that needs to be given special attention.

7. IS security policy and maintenance theme

Information security policies provide a framework for best practice that can be followed by all employees. They help to ensure risk is minimized and that any security incidents are effectively responded to. Information security policies will also help turn staff into participants in the company's efforts to secure its information assets, and the process of developing these policies will help to define a company's information assets. Information security policy defines the organization's attitude to information, and announces internally and externally that information is an asset, the property of the organization, and is to be protected from unauthorized access, modification, disclosure and destruction.

IS security policy can be used to help banks ensure they have the controls in place to work towards compliance by mapping policy statements to legislative requirements. In this way they can provide evidence that their baseline security controls are in line with regulations and legislation. Therefore banking industries in Ethiopia need to establish and implement an approved IS security policy through policy enforcement in order to reduce the risk of unauthorized disclosure, alteration and destruction of sensitive information of their banks.

The established IS security policy should incorporate ethical conduct policy, technical aspects (physical and logical security), organizational aspects etc. In addition to the establishment of the policy, banks of Ethiopia should review and update their security policy periodically in order to create a commonly held and shared IS culture throughout the bank.

The main requirements of IS security policy and maintenance theme is defined as follows:
- Establish and implement an approved IS security policy for the bank.
- Develop IS security procedures, guidelines, manuals etc. for the bank.
- Review and update IS security policy periodically.
- Enforce IS security policy throughout the bank.

8. Collaboration work theme

In order to assure the confidentiality, availability and integrity of data's which is found in the banking industry of Ethiopia, a tough cooperation and collaboration work is needed within the banks departments/offices/divisions/teams. Therefore, a collaboration work between IT department, IT security office or division and IT audit division or team is highly needed in order to assure the IS security process of the bank works effectively and complies with the security policy and regulation of the bank in order to maximize the protection of the bank's asset and information.

The main requirements of collaboration work theme is defined as follows:
- IT department must communicate and collaborate with IT security office in order to assure the confidentiality, availability and integrity of the bank's asset or information.
- IT security office must communicate and collaborate with IT audit division in order to evaluate the IS security practices or processes of the bank and to ensure that controls are functioning as intended.
- IT department must communicate and collaborate with IT audit division in order to assure whether the IT department and its operations comply with the IS security policy of the bank. IT audit division ensures IS security compliance.

9. IS security ownership theme

All employees (staffs) of the bank must be trained and aware in their information systems security responsibilities and are held accountable. As a result it is important for staff of the banks of Ethiopia to understand their security roles and responsibilities in order to enhance their security performance and also their bank's performance. By understanding their responsibilities and the importance of protecting information, staffs are able to understand what security risks are associated with their actions. This will increase their security awareness levels, which will increase compliance with the IS security policy of the bank. Similarly author in [55] attempts to conclude that employee responsibility and ownership of the need to protect information security is an important aspect of creating a security culture in the organization.

By being responsible and having a sense of ownership staff behavior will change with respect to protecting the banks assets leads to the creation of a commonly held and shared IS security culture within the banks of Ethiopia.

The main requirements of IS security ownership theme can be defined as follows:
- Train and aware all the bank staffs about their IS security roles and responsibilities.
- Enforce the IS security policy of the bank.

Inter dependencies of the main activities of the system is also described in the table shown below:

Table 5.1 List of inter dependent activities for modeling Information systems security system

Activities	Dependencies	Explanation
1		To create a security culture within Ethiopian banks top management support and involvement is crucial in implementing an effective IS security practice within the bank.
2	1	To restructure or develop a structure of IT security office to report directly to the CEO, top management must involve and approve the new structure.
3	1	IT/IS security steering committee serves as an effective communication channel for management's aims and directions and provides an ongoing basis for ensuring alignment of the security programme with organizational objectives. Therefor top management must establish IT security steering committee for the bank.
4	3,6,7	In order to communicate IS security policy to the staff throughout the bank, in order to communicate IT security steering committee to the bank about the IS security program, in order to conduct IS security awareness throughout the bank there must be an effective communication mechanism.
5	3	To give adequate training and education for IT security experts, IT security steering committee must identify and allocate adequate IS security resources like sufficient budget.
6	3	In order to conduct IS security awareness throughout the bank, IT security steering committee should first implement IS security program.
7	3,1	To implement, enforce and maintain IS security policy throughout the bank, IT security must review and provide to the top management for approve and top management must approve the IS security policy.
8	1	In order to create a strong consistent collaboration work within the three business units (IT department, IT security office and IT audit division) top management must establish a collaboration work.
9	5,6,7	In order to create a security ownership among all staffs of the bank, conducting IS security awareness, providing education and training, and implementing IS security policy through enforcement must be undertaken.

After identifying the relationships the author of this research design a conceptual model as shown in the figure below:

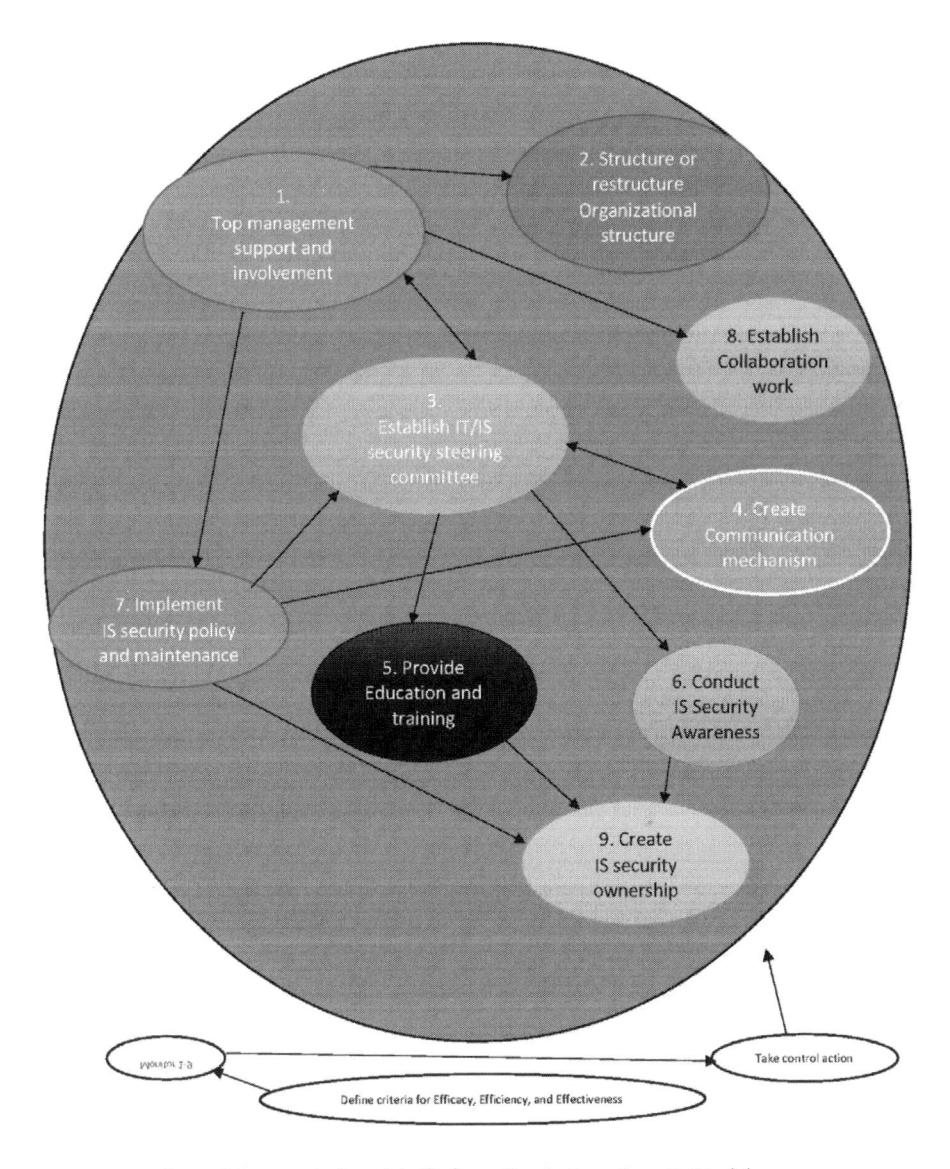

Figure 5.2 conceptual model of Information Systems Security Model

5.5 Evaluation (comparison of the model with the rich picture)

In this section a comparison of the conceptual model which is developed in stage 4 (four) of the approach (SSM) in which this research uses as a tool for developing the framework with the rich picture developed in stage 2 (two) and the expressed problem obtained from the survey (questionnaire and interview findings) were discussed in order to improve the problem situation.

Comparison of the model with the real world problem: stage five

During this stage the developed conceptual model from the root definitions is compared against the problematic situation in order to define the required improvement areas or changes. In support of the above sentences comparison of the conceptual model with real world or what should happen with what actually happens. A comparison is to test where the differences and similarities lie.

According to Checkland's recommendation there are four ways of comparing the model with the real world problem situation. The author of this research choose and adopts the most common comparison type of Checkland's recommendation, which is "a structured questioning of the model using a matrix approach" that looks at each activities of the model and ask questions like: does it exist in the real world, how does it behave, how is its performance identified and measured, and is this process any good. The author of this research uses the activities of the conceptual model as a source of questions for conducting a debate or discussion among the key stakeholders or participants to set a recommendation about what changes are needed to solve, improve or enhance the existing problem.

After conducting a discussion with the key participants (SSM group) about the comparison, the author of this research try to combine and integrate the key participant's (SSM group) idea and come up with an accommodation of their recommendations (comments) in order to improve the existing problem. To simplify and clearly state this kind of comparison an accommodation of participant's idea for change has been constructed for each activity and each sub-activities of the system which are presented in the table below.

Table 5.2 comparison of the conceptual model with the expressed problem situation

Activities and sub-activities in conceptual model (stage four)	Present in real world situation	Comments (proposed change activities)
Top management support and involvement		
i. place IS security in the Board's agenda	Partially	CEO should place the IS security on the Board's agenda in order to get attention from the Boards.
ii. identify and assign IT security leaders, hold them accountable	Partially	Top management should assign IT security manager and hold them accountable to ensure the overall IS security activities of the bank.
iii. Assign IS security to a key committee and ensure adequate support.	Not available	Top management should assign IT security steering committee from the concerned business units of the bank.
iv. Establish and allocate responsibilities for IS security risk management of the bank.	Not available	Top management should establish and allocate responsibilities for IS security risk management of the bank. Top management and Board of directors should or must give a direction on how to build and implement adequate risk management process of the bank.
v. Approve new or existing IS security policy.	Present	
Organizational structure		
i. Develop or restructure IT security office to report directly to the CEO or president of the bank.	Partially	Top management of Ethiopian banks should develop or restructure IT security office to report directly to the CEO or president of the bank.
ii. Empower the IT security office with sufficient authority.	Partially	What empowers IT security is its independence when it's granted through charter. After the restructuring the organizational structure top management or CEO should approve the charter for the IT security office.

Page | 71

IT/IS security steering committee		
i. Establish IT security steering committee that have actors from the concerned department and executives.	There is no IT/IS security steering committee in the banks of Ethiopia.	IT security steering committee should be established and organized at each banks of Ethiopia.
a. Communicate the IS security program to the bank.	Not available	The bank must develop IS security program. And then the IT security steering committee should communicate the IS security program to the bank.
b. Communicate the importance of IS security objectives and the need for continual improvement	Not available	IT security steering committee should communicate to the top management of the bank about the importance of IS security objectives and the need for continual improvement.
c. Communicate IS security breaches and incidents to the bank staff and to public.	Not available	Communicating IS security breaches and incidents to the public is not culturally feasible in the context of Ethiopian people's awareness about overall IS security activities and processes.
d. Determine and allocate IS security resources	Partially available, tools and trainings are very scarce	IT/IS security steering committee should or must determine and allocate IS security resources adequately and effectively.
e. Coordinate the creation of IS security incident management team.	Not available	IT security incident management has to establish and implement in the bank. Therefore IT security steering committee should coordinate on the creation of IS security incident management team.
f. Implements IS security training and awareness program.	Not practiced	IT/IS security steering committee must implement IS security awareness and training program. The awareness plan should incorporate and the password and password related activities and should incorporate business continuity as a key area to communicate to the staff of the bank.
g. Provides approval of new or existing IS security policies.	Not available	IT security steering committee should provide the new or existing IS security policy to the top management for approval.

ii. To provide and use effective decision technique.	Not practiced, to deliver this kind of activity IS/IT security steering committee should be established first	IT security steering committee should provide and use effective decision techniques for ensuring the alignment of IS security with the bank's objectives. The committee help in making a decision on the bank's IS security activities and processes.
Communication		
i. Define information and knowledge needs to be shared.	Not practiced	The bank should or must clearly define information and knowledge that needs to be shared among and within the bank.
ii. Define IS security policy needs to be communicated to the staff.	Not practiced	IT security office and its experts should clearly define the IS security policy that needs to be communicated to the staff.
iii. Identify staff applications that are needed.	Not practiced	IT security office should clearly identify staff application that needs special protection in order to conduct a focus based and application based IS security awareness training.
iv. Identify IS security incidents and breaches needs to be shared to the public.	Not practiced	It is a good practice, but according to Ethiopian people's awareness on IS security it is not culturally feasible.
v. Deliver an effective communication mechanism.	Not practiced	Communicating effectively is one important aspects to address staff. Therefore the bank should deliver an effective mechanism.
Education and training		
i. Provide sufficient tools for IT security experts.	Not practiced	To build an effective IS security it is a must to provide necessary tools. Therefore the bank must provide a sufficient tools for the IT security experts.
ii. Supply instruction guidance and manuals that can be easily understood.	Not practiced	IT security office should supply instruction guidance and manuals to the staff of the bank that can be easily understood.
iii. Offer suitable IS security courses to cover specific topics.	Not practiced	A dedicated training for security office is a must. Therefore the bank (IT/IS security steering

		committee) must allocate enough budget for the IT security office and offer suitable/advanced training for IT security experts.
iv. Provide well trained lecturers.	Not practiced	The bank should provide a well-trained and certified lecturers.
Awareness		
i. Conduct a cased-based awareness for the top management about IS security breaches and incidents.	Not practiced	IT security office must conduct a cased-based awareness for the top management about IS security breaches, frauds and incidents to get their buy in and to increase their IS security awareness level.
ii. Conduct an ongoing and continuous IS security awareness throughout the bank.	Partially	IT security office must conduct an ongoing and continuous IS security awareness throughout the bank.
iii. Conduct a group or focused-based and role based IS security awareness.	Not practiced	Non-technical staff of Ethiopian banks were more negative than IT staffs on IS security activities. Therefore IT security office must conduct a focused IS security awareness training session and role-based responsibilities of security training.
IS security policy and maintenance		
i. Establish and implement an approved IS security policy.	Partially	IT security office must establish and implement an IS security policy in the bank.
ii. Develop IS security procedures, guidelines, manuals etc.	Not practiced	IT security office must develop IS security procedures, guidelines, manuals etc. that can be easily understood by the staff of the bank.
iii. Enforce IS security policy.	Partially	IT security office must enforce IS security policy of the bank and request on non-compliance.
iv. Review and update IS security policy periodically.	Partially	IT security office must review and update IS security policy and should present to the top management for approval.

Collaboration work		
i. Establish a cooperation and collaboration work between IT department and IT security office.	Partially present	Top management should establish a cooperation and collaboration work among IT security office and IT department in order to implement effective IS security controls to assure the confidentiality, availability and integrity of the bank's data.
ii. Establish a cooperation and collaboration work between IT security office and IT audit division.	Partially present	Top management should establish a cooperation and collaboration work among IT security office and IT audit division in order to evaluate overall IS security practices or processes of the bank and to ensure that controls are functioning as intended.
iii. Establish a cooperation and collaboration work between IT department and IT audit division.	Partially present	IT department must communicate and cooperate with IT audit division in order to assure whether the IT department and its operations comply with the IS security policy of the bank.
IS security ownership		
i. Aware all staffs about their IS security role and responsibilities.	Not practiced	IT security office must aware all the staff of the bank about their IS security roles and responsibilities continuously throughout the bank in order to create IS security ownership among all staffs of the bank.
ii. Enforce IS security policy.	Partially	IT security office must enforce IS security policy throughout the bank to create security ownership among all staffs of the bank.

Culturally feasible and systematically desirable changes: stage six

At this stage the result obtained from stage five leads into a discussion of things as they are now currently versus things as they might be in the future after change. The author of this research conducts a discussions with the five relevant participants (SSM group) involved in this research. The discussion result helps to come up with an accepted and common ideas and suggest the possible changes. These changes were agreed by key participants (SSM group) to be systematically desirable and culturally feasible. In this research attitudinal, structural and procedural changes were addressed using the SSM approach.

The survey and discussion with the participant of SSM shows that convincing top management about the importance of IS security is almost none in the banking industry of Ethiopia, therefore changes suggested by the SSM group in the banks of Ethiopia is necessary. The main change to solve this kind of problem is conducting an awareness about IS security objectives to the top management is very essential in order to get their attention, because top managements are the ones who have the most influence in the bank. The awareness plan or program must focus on business benefit that can be gained from improving IS security activities of the bank, IS security breaches and incidents happened in recent times in order to convince the top management of the banks of Ethiopia by align IS security objectives with the business objective of the banks. Another change suggested by the SSM group is conducting a continuous IS security awareness and training for all staffs of the bank is a must activity, the awareness and training plan should incorporate business continuity as one of the key areas to be communicated to staffs, should focus on the practical usage of information security controls and should also considers a focused training session for specific groups who needs special attention. These change are attitudinal.

Top management support and involvement is also the main activity for the success of effective implementation of IS security activity and process in the bank. This activity is also accepted and suggested by the SSM group discussion as a primary change in the banking industry. The main activities of top management support are: place IS security on the boards agenda, identify and assign IT security leaders hold them accountable and ensure support for them, assign IS security to a key committee and ensure adequate support for them, define and allocate responsibilities for IS security risk management activities and process of the bank, particularly for acceptance residual risks, and approve new or existing IS security policy. These changes are procedural.

Another area of possible change in the banking industries in Ethiopia suggested by the SSM group discussion is organizational structure of IT security office. Organizational structure is also defines how activities such as task allocation, coordination and supervision are directed toward the achievement of organizational aim. The most important thing here in IS security is to avoid conflict of interest, which is separation of the operation from control and audit. IT security office or division should have an appropriate power in order to implement and control IS security activities and processes of the banks. Therefore IT security office should report to directly to the CEO or president of the bank. These changes are structural.

Result obtained from the discussion and data collected shows that there is no IT security steering committee in Ethiopian industry. Discussion in the SSM group strongly suggested the need to establish IT/IS security steering committee that have actors from the concerned department and executives of the banks of Ethiopia. Information Systems security steering committee serves as an effective communication channel for management's aim and directions and provides an ongoing basis for insuring alignment of the security program with the organizational objectives. The main activities of IT/IS security steering committee are: communicate the IS security program to the bank, communicate the importance of IS security objectives and continual improvement, communicate IS security breaches and incidents to the bank staff, monitor and measure the IS security risk management of the bank, define and allocate IS security resources like provide sufficient budget for the IT security office can help the office to conduct IS security awareness throughout the bank effectively and efficiently, tools, peoples (hire IT security experts and train the existing IT security staffs) etc. these changes are also structural.

It has been manifest from group discussion and data collected (questionnaire and interview findings) that banking industry in Ethiopia have encountered a problem in establishing and implementing IS security policy, which is the policy is likely informal and most of the time it is not approved by the top management. As the SSM group discussion agreed and suggested a change in procedure is that establish and implement IS security policy, guidelines, procedure, manuals etc. throughout policy enforcement, review and update the policy periodically. These changes are procedural.

It has been marked from group discussion and data collected (questionnaire and interview findings) that banks in Ethiopia are weak in providing an advanced education and training for the IT security experts. Changes in this case has been suggested as follows: banks of Ethiopia should provide sufficient tools and facilitates for the IT security experts, supply instruction guidance and manuals that can be easily understood, and provide well trained lecturers. These changes are procedural.

It has been evident from group discussion and data collected (questionnaire and interview findings) that banking industry in Ethiopia are weak in delivering an effective communication mechanism within the bank. The SSM group discussion agreed on an acceptable idea and suggested that Banks in Ethiopia should deliver a strong and consistent communication mechanisms for communicating IS security policy, procedures, guidelines, manuals etc. throughout the bank effectively and efficiently. Managements should communicate to their staffs about IS security requirements. These communication mechanisms can be workshop, through the bank's intranet, through the bank's e-mail, web-based training and so on. These changes are procedural.

Another finding has been also shown that in Ethiopian banks the collaboration work among the business units within the bank is not strong. As the SSM group discussion suggested that it is feasible for the top managements of the bank to establish a strong and consistent cooperation and collaboration work among the three business units of the bank. The three business units of the bank which needs a collaboration work effort are IT department, IT security office and IT audit division. These changes are procedural.

The survey and discussion with the participants of the SSM group have shown that creating a security ownership among the all staffs is not practiced in banking industries of Ethiopia. IS security is not only the responsibilities of top management, IT security steering committee, or IT security office rather it the responsibilities of all employees of the bank. As the participants of the SSM group discussion suggested that it is a must criteria to aware and train all staffs of the bank about their IS security roles and responsibilities continuously to hold them accountable in order to enhance their security performance and their bank's performance. By understanding their responsibilities and the importance of protecting information, staffs are able to understand what security risks are associated with their action. In addition to the above changes the bank's IT security office must also enforce IS security policy and request for non-compliance. The above two changes suggested by the participants will increase the staffs awareness level, which will also increase compliance with the IS security policy of the bank. These changes are procedural.

To conclude that all the nine main human activities of the conceptual model are agreed, accepted and suggested by the key participants (SSM group) to be systemically desirable and culturally feasible except that two sub-activities of the conceptual model have been omitted, the reason why the two sub-activities of the conceptual model omitted is that they are systemically desirable but culturally not feasible in the context of Ethiopian peoples IS security awareness. Because of the poor maturity of the awareness level of the people and absence of regulatory organ in publicizing IS security breaches and incidents, customers will totally shift their money to another bank who have not publicize IS security breaches and incidents.

The author of this research commissioned the research by selecting the problem initially, but it is not in a position to take action as a result of it. This research ends with stage six of the SSM, Checkland also [58] pointed out: *"Some studies will be ended after defining the action, some after implementing it."* Ethiopian banking industry management bodies may take action when they become aware of this research but the author of this research is not required to do so and also the researcher is not in a position to take action as a result of it. Therefore the final stage of SSM which is stage seven is omitted in this research.

5.6 Discussion

The author of this research obtained a clear picture through a discussion with the key participants (SSM group) and data collected (questionnaire and interview) at each site of the surveyed banks of Ethiopia. This research clearly identifies IS security issues and challenges occurred in banks of Ethiopia which are: absence of IT security steering committee, communication gap with the management and staff, lack of IS security awareness, lack of financial and human (IS security qualified experts) resource, lack of IS security governance, inefficiency of IS security risk management processes, lack of advanced training for IT security experts, disorganization of IT security office in the organizational structure, and implementation of informal and unapproved IS security policy in the banking industry in Ethiopia.

In this research by using the approach (SSM), the author has been identified social and political issues and obstacles found in the Ethiopian banks like: lack of IS security awareness, high level of power distance cultural factor within the top management and IT security office of the bank resulted a challenge in order to convince and aware top management of the banks of Ethiopia about the importance and necessity of IS security objectives in safeguarding the banks data and the need for continual improvement, lack of policy enforcement due to lack of IT security office empowerment and so on.

5.7 Summary

In this chapter the author of this research discusses the rationale for using the approach (Soft Systems Methodology), apply six stages of SSM, explore the IS security problems, conflicts and issues that are facing in Ethiopian banking industries using rich picture. The rich picture is constructed from the detailed information gathered through the process of un-structured interview and discussion with the people involved in the SSM groups (five relevant participants). Results are discussed analysed, finally conclusions are drawn from the result obtained.

Summary of the surveys (questionnaire and interview findings) were discussed and presented in order to help the researcher to integrate and combine the rich picture with the summary of the surveys to clearly identify the main activities and to define the root definition of the relevant system of the expressed problem situation which exists in the banking industry in Ethiopia. The main reason why the author combines the survey findings with the rich picture is, as we know the approach (SSM) in this research participates only 5 peoples (SSM participants) in order to explore the problem situation (rich picture) faced in the surveyed banks of Ethiopia. It seems inefficient to conclude or generalize the expressed problem (rich picture) is effective and adequate in expressing the problem situation happened in the real world of Ethiopian banks in IS security aspect. Therefore the author conducts a semi-structured interview for 15 peoples and distribute 150 questionnaire and get 129 adequate response in order to get an in-depth and a deep understanding of the problem from different stakeholder's point of view from the surveyed banks of Ethiopia.

The author identifies nine (9) logical model of human activities and processes that must be carried out in order to satisfy the root definition that are relevant to the system. At last the author develops a conceptual model (Information Systems Security Model) for the expressed problem in the banking industries in Ethiopia.

After developing the conceptual model the author compare the conceptual model with the expressed real world problem situation in order to achieve possible changes suggested by participants of the SSM group to identify and define systemically desirable and culturally feasible changes to improve the problem situation.

CHAPTER SIX
CONCLUSION AND RECOMMENDATION

6.1 Conclusion

The main purpose of IS security is to protect information and specifically to assure the confidentiality, integrity and availability of data through an organizations network and telecommunication channels. Maintaining IS security requires support cooperation from all employees within the organization, even though technical aspect of IS security needs due attention a more serious and under rated aspect of IS security is the human element.

Different literatures and empirical studies have revealed that focusing on the technical aspect of IS security without due consideration of how human interacts with the system is clearly insufficient in safeguarding an organizational sensitive information. The main aim of this research is investigate and identify the human element rather than the technical aspect of IS security, therefore in investigating a human aspect and social activities of the organization SSM is the best choice of from other approaches.

Human based threats, natural disaster threats, and technology threats are major threats of banking industry, this research adopts a broader perspective and presents an understanding of IS security in terms of a social and organizational perspective by using the Checkland's Soft Systems Methodology as an approach in order to achieve a greater insight of the problem situation and with the aim of identifying changes which could improve it. The aim of this research is to develop Information Systems Security Model for Ethiopian banking industry using Soft System approach by perceiving dynamic behavior of the human aspect and holistic view of information security practices in the Ethiopian banking industry.

The main reasons why the author of this research adopts SSM as an approaches is it is practical, highly participative, used as a learning tool and flexible approach to manage changes by perceiving a holistic approach that takes a wider range of factors into account including social and political aspects aiming to suggest change that is meaningful and feasible in the organizational context. In addition as defined by Checkland SSM is not a system development methodology rather it is a methodology to identify changes and also it is a human problem oriented and SSM also it is a process oriented not technique oriented. A number of models can be built to represent different viewpoints of different stakeholders and exploration of problem situations are used to decide an action for desirable changes.

Applying the SSM enabled the author of this research to capture the different attitude and conception of stakeholders about IS security practices within the banks. Another strength of SSM in this research is that it enabled the researcher to capture and identify vulnerabilities related to some stakeholders' attitude, for instance the high level of power distance culture factor innate in the bank of Ethiopia, the rich picture of the problem situation has revealed issue related to security awareness. Also another strength of SSM is used to gain learning, for instance in comparison of ideal system with the real problem the participants can perceive their own idea and understand another's perspective to come up with an accepted or an accommodation of possible changes.

This research used a survey in the form of questionnaire and interview with the combination of another unstructured interview for the purpose of conducting a discussion with the key participants (SSM group) for creating a rich picture of the problem situation, for developing a root definition of the relevant system and for suggesting a desirable and feasible change. The reason why this research uses the first survey (questionnaire and semi-structured interview) is to a response for the research questions and to avoid the limitation of the SSM in which this research adopts as an approach. Since SSM lacks to generalize the solution when the population of the surveyed banks get bigger which is 5 banks of Ethiopia, because the researcher uses 5 participants for applying the SSM process. As a result 150 questionnaires were distributed to the surveyed banks of Ethiopia in order to get an understanding of there IS security knowledge and awareness level of the staffs (technical and non-technical) of the bank and an interview is conducted to a total of 15 selected staffs of the surveyed banks of Ethiopia in order to get un in-depth understanding of the IS problems facing in their banks.

Finally the author of this research combine and integrates the summary of the survey with the rich picture of the expressed problem situation and then develops and propose a conceptual model using the Soft systems Methodology. In the meantime the IT security managers' report of their evaluation result of the approach (SSM) as they investigate it when participating in developing IS security system, they found the approach satisfactory, desirable and culturally feasible in the context of banking industries in Ethiopia, easily usable by the banks of Ethiopia as a baseline, testable, it is comprehensive and complete, enriched by literatures, and can be easily maintainable by other practitioners.

6.2 Solutions and Recommendations

Possible recommendations which are systemically desirable and culturally feasible solutions for the situation are proposed for Ethiopian banking industries.

For this research, in terms of seeking accommodation among this group of people (five representatives whose positions are high in their respective banks) who have different worldviews (the "W"), and potential solutions (the "T") to this situation, and to have a common concern (concern of implementing information systems security model), thus solutions should be developed with a consideration that these people could probably all feel acceptable. Moreover, based on the result of the "seven stages" of SSM and the model mapping, a solution could also be developed to be "systemically desirable" and "culturally feasible", which means these solutions derived from the "relevant systems" need to be in fact perceived to be truly relevant and will alleviate some of the problems, and also the actors within the system will be inclined to engage with the changes proposed and the change process itself [11, 47].

Conducting an awareness about IS security objectives to the top management is very essential in order to get top management's attention, because top managements are the ones who have the most influence in the bank. IT Security Office of Ethiopian banks should conduct IS security awareness. The awareness plan or program must focus on business benefit that can be gained from improving IS security activities of the bank.

Top management support and involvement is also the main activity for the success of effective implementation of IS security activity and process in the bank. This activity is also accepted and suggested by the SSM group discussion as a primary change in the banking industries.

Another area of possible change in the banking industries in Ethiopia suggested by the SSM group discussion is organizational structure of IT security office. IT security office should report to directly to the President or Chief Executive Officer of the bank.

Result obtained from the discussion and data collected shows that there is no IT security steering committee in Ethiopian industry. Discussion in the SSM group strongly suggested the need to establish IT/IS security steering committee that have actors from the concerned department and executives of the banks of Ethiopia.

It has been manifest from group discussion and data collected (questionnaire and interview findings) that banking industry in Ethiopia have encountered a problem in implementing and enforcing IS security policy. As the SSM group discussion agreed and suggested a change in procedure is that establish and implement IS security policy, guidelines, procedure, manuals etc. throughout policy enforcement, review and update the policy periodically.

It has been marked from group discussion and data collected (questionnaire and interview findings) that banks in Ethiopia are weak in providing an advanced education and training for the IT security experts. Therefore, banks of Ethiopia should provide sufficient tools and facilitates information security related trainings for the IT security experts, supply instruction guidance and manuals that can be easily understood, and provide well trained lecturers.

SSM group discussion agreed on an acceptable idea and suggested that Banks in Ethiopia should deliver a strong and consistent communication mechanisms for communicating IS security policy, procedures, guidelines, manuals etc.

As the SSM group discussion suggested that it is feasible for the top managements of the bank to establish a strong and consistent cooperation and collaboration work among the three business units of the bank. The three business units of the bank which needs a collaboration work effort are IT department, IT security office and IT audit division. These changes are procedural.

As the participants of the SSM group discussion suggested that it is a must criteria to aware and train all staffs of the bank about their IS security roles and responsibilities continuously to hold them accountable in order to enhance their security performance and their bank's performance.

When banks in Ethiopia wants to develop and implement information systems security framework or baseline for their banks, it is recommended they consider following issues:

1. Top management support and involvement
2. Structuring or restructuring Organizational structure of IT security office
3. Establishing IT/IS security steering committee for the bank.
4. Creating a Communication mechanism throughout the bank.
5. Provide adequate education and training for IT security experts.
6. Conduct IS security awareness.
7. Implement IS security policy through policy enforcement.
8. Establish a collaboration work with three business units (IT security office, IT audit division and IT/IS department).

The following recommendations are presented as possible ways to improve this research are:

- As the author of this research tried to convince that the stage 7 of SSM in this research has been omitted for the defined reason in section 5.5 the researcher commissioned the research by selecting the problem initially, but it is not in a position to take action as a result of it. Therefore, further research for the topic of the research can be conducted after implemented solutions and the SSM process could start again. This will help practitioners to conduct further research on this topic of the research.

- The research showed that where staffs and other stakeholders, who can influence the outcome of change, can be engaged in the SSM process, building an accommodation of views and an understanding of the change process could enhance the rate of change. This produced new knowledge on the application of soft systems methodology. This will contribute to a learning.

- This research may be an initial point for practitioners and researchers who want to conduct more comprehensive research in this area from Ethiopian banks perspective.

REFERENCES

[1]. Lee, A.S. Thinking about social theory and philosophy for information systems. John Willey and Sons, Ltd, Chichester, England, 2004, pp1-26.

[2]. Dhillon, G. Principles of information systems security: text and cases Willey 2007.

[3]. Baskerville, R.: Risk Analysis: An Interpretive Feasibility Tool in Justifying Information Systems Security, European Journal of Information Systems, Vol. 1, No. 2, 121-130. (1991).

[4]. Von Solms, "information security – the fourth wave", journal of Elsevier computers and security 25 (2006), 165-168.

[5]. Martins and Eloff, "Information Security culture in public hospitals: the case of Hawassa referral hospital", the African journal of information systems, vol.3, issue 3, 2011, pp.72-86.

[6]. www.gov.uk/government/uploads/system/uploads/attachment_data/file/244978/bis-13-1206-network-and-information-security-directive-impactassessment.pdf.

[7]. PwC (PricewaterhouseCooper) 2014 Annual Global CEO Survey.

[8]. Abiy Woretaw and Lemma Lessa, "information security culture in the banking sector in Ethiopia" 5th ICT 2012 Ethiopian conference June 08, 2012, 22 page.

[9]. Checkland P. Systems Thinking, Systems Practice, 1989. John willey: Chichester

[10]. Checkland P. Systems Thinking, Systems Practice, 1999, Wiley, ISBN 0-471-98606-2

[11]. Checkland, p. and Scholes J. 1990. Soft systems methodology in action. John willey: Chichester.

[12]. Vroom, C. and von Solms, R. 2004. Towards information security behavioral compliance. Computers and security, 23 (3):191-198.

[13]. Schneider, B. Secrets & Lies: Digital Security in a Networked World, John Wiley & Sons, 2000.

[14]. Parsons K, McCormack T, Butavicius M, and Ferguson L. human factors and information security: individual culture and security environment. Defense science and technology organization. October 2010.pp 1-45

[15]. Siponen, M. and Oinas –Kukkonen, H. 2007. A review of information security issues and respective research contribution. SIGMIS database, 38(1):60-80

[16]. Dhillon and Torkzadeh. 2006. value-focus assessment of information systems security in organizations. Information system journals, 16:293-314.

[17]. Jabiri Kuwe Bakari, Charles N. Tarimo, Louise Yngstrom, Christer Magnusson, Stewart Kowalski, "Bridging the gap between general management and technicians – A case study on ICT security in developing country" , journal of Elsevier computers & security 26 (2007) , 44–55.

[18]. Munirul Ula, Zuraini BT Ismail and Zailani Mohamed Sidek, "A framework for the governance of information security in banking system", journal of information assurance and cyber security, vol.2011 (2011), article ID 72619, 12 pages.

[19]. Ioannis Koskosas, Konstantinos Kakoulidis, Christos Siomos, "Information Security: corporate culture and organizational commitment", international journal of humanities and social science, vol.1, no.3, 192-198, March 2011.

[20]. Saleh Al Zhrani, Al Imam Muhammad bin Saud University, Riyadh, Saudi Arabia "development of a soft system model to identify information and communications technology issues and obstacles in governmental organization in Saudi Arabia", Journal of Theoretical and Applied Information Technology, pp. 93-104.

[21]. Umoh, Godwin I. And Ndu, Eugene C. International Journal of Business and Business Management Review. Vol.1, No. 3, pp. 111-127, September 2013.
[22]. Ker linger. 1986. Foundation of behavioral design. Pp.279.
[23]. Greene, J.C., Caracelli, V.J. and Graham, W.F. 1989. Toward a conceptual framework for mixed method evaluation design. Educational evaluation and policy analysis, 11(3), 255-274
[24]. Creswell, J.W. 2005. Educational research: planning, conducting and evaluating quantitative and qualitative research (second edition). Upper saddle river, NJ: person education
[25]. Creswell, J.W., and Plano Clark. 2007. Designing and conducting mixed method research. Thousand Oaks, CA; sage.
[26]. Checkland p., "system thinking, systems practice: includes a 30 years retrospective", ISBN 978-0471-98606-5, 424 pages, July 1999.
[27]. The 10th cryptographers' track at the RSA conference 2010, San Francisco, CA, USA March 1-5, 2010. Proceedings.
[28]. IT Governance Institution. Publication "Information Security Governance: guidance for Boards of Directors and Executive Management 2nd edition" cobit 4.1. USA. 2007.
[29]. Jtc 1/SC 27, "ISO/IEC 27000:2009, information security management system-overview and vocabulary," the International Organization for Standardization and the International Eletrotechnical Commission, standard 2009.
[30]. Dhillon, G. and Mishra, S. Information systems security governance research: a behavioral perspective. Virginia Commonwealth University: pp.18-26.
[31]. Jtc 1/SC 27, "ISO/IEC 27000:2009, information security management system-overview and vocabulary," the International Organization for Standardization and the International Eletrotechnical Commission, standard 2006.
[32]. Troy Leach, chief standards architect "PCI security standard council: standards 2.0 overview", November 2010.
[33]. James P. Councill, III. Mayor 621 Hunterdale Road, Franklin, VA 23851. October 3 2006.
[34]. Akhmed Syakhroza (2003). Best practice corporate governance dalam konteks local per Banka Indonesia. Majalah Usahaulan. (Online), no.06 th.xxII, 8 halaman.tersedia: https://www. lmfeui/uploads/file26-xxII-juni-2001.pdf
[35]. Alemayehu Geda (2006), "the structure and performance of Ethiopia's financial sector in the pre and post reform period. With special focus on banking", United Nation University, World Institute For Development Economic Research (UNU-WIDER), working paper, no.2006/112.
[36]. Belay Geday (1990), "money, banking and insurance in Ethiopia", Addis Ababa berhaneselam printing press (in Amharic).
[37]. A.Bilal, K.Stewart. "Security from a system thinking perspective: applying SSM to the analysis of information security incident". Stockholm University. P.17.
[38]. Yegidis, B.L. & Weinbach, R.W. (1996). Research Methods for social workers. (2nd edition). Boston: Allyn & Bacon.
[39]. Martins, A. & Eloff, J.H.B. 2002. "Information security culture" in proceeding of the international conference on information security, Cairo, Egypt.
[40]. Anene I., Nnolim, Annette L., Steenkamp, in proceedings of the 6th annual ISOnEworld conference, April 11-13, 200, Las Vegas, NV, 9 pages.

[41]. A. Martins, "information security culture" unpublished PHD thesis, Rand Africans University (2002).
[42]. A Da Viega and J. Eloff, "a framework and assessment instrument for information security culture," computers and security, vol 29, no 2, (2010) March, pp. 196-207.
[43]. Internet: www.festo.com/catalogue/subject to change 2017/01.
[44]. Checkland, P., and Winter, M. 2006. Process and content: two ways of using SSM. Journal of the operational research society 57 (12), 1435-1441.
[45]. Al-Zahrani, S. 2001, Computer Network System for University Hospitals in Saudi Arabia, PhD thesis, Loughborough University.
[46]. Ledington P.W.J. & Ledington J. the problem of comparison in soft systems methodology, systems research and behavioral science, 16, 329-339.
[47]. Warwick, J. (2008). A case study using a soft sytems methodology in the evolution of mathematics module. The montana mathematics enthusiast, 5(2&3), 269-290.
[48]. Cecez-Keemanovic, D., Kautz, K., and Abrahal, R. 2014. "Reframing success and failure of Information Systems: a performative perspective," MIS quarterly (38:2), pp.561-588.
[49]. Jagodzinki, j. (2002). A strange introduction: my apple thing. In j.jagodzinski (ED), pedagocial desire: authority, seduction, transferes, and the question of ethics, (pp.v-ix). Westport, CT: Bergin and Garvey.
[50]. Atkinson, C., 2000. The 'soft information systems and technology methodology': an actor contingency approach to integrate development. Eur. J. inform.syst.9, 104-123.
[51]. Bausch, K.C. "Roots and branches: a brief, picaresque, personal history of systems theory", Systems Research and Behavioral Science (19:5), September 2002, pp. 417428.
[52]. Checkland PB. And Holwell SE, 2006, 'The processes which information systems support', in Introducing Information Management: the business approach, (eds) Hinton M, Elsevier, London, New York and Amsterdam, pp 63-74
[53]. Kurbanoglu, A., 1992. Planning an information network for Turkey: A system study. PhD thesis, Sheffield University.
[54]. Koh, Ruighaver, A. B., Maynard, S. B., & Ahmad, A. (2005). *Security Governance: Its Impact on Security Culture*.
[55]. Chellappan P, Ramachandran V, Pita JS and Fauquet CM "Short-interfering RNA accumulation correlates with host recovery in DNA virus infected hosts, and gene silencing targets specific viral sequences"*Journal of Virology* 78 7465-7477. 2002.
[56]. Checkland, p., & Poulter, J. (2010). Soft systems methodology.in.M.Reynolds & S.Holwell (EDs), systems approach to managing change. A practical guide (pp. 191-242). London: Springer-Verlag.
[57]. Shemlse.G, "Information Systems Security Audit Framework for Banking Industry", July 2013, Thesis, reviewed from HiLCoE school of computer science and technology library, Addis Ababa, Ethiopia.
[58]. Aychiluhim.D, "Internet Banking Security Framework: the case of Ethiopian Banking Industry", May 2014, Thesis, reviewed from HiLCoE school of computer science and technology library, Addis Ababa, Ethiopia.

[59]. Yigezzu.B, "Information Systems Security Audit readiness in case of Ethiopian government organization", 2011, retrieved from http://www.spidercenter.org/sites/default/files/master_thesissponsored/Ms_Thesis_Yigezzujorro.pdf.
[60]. A.Gemech, "Adoption of Electronic Banking System in Ethiopian Banking Industry: Barriers and Drivers", May 14, 2012, retrieved from http://www.papers.ssrn.com/so13/papers.cfm?abstract_id=2058202.
[61]. Balcha.R, "State of Cyber Security in Ethiopia", Tune 2012, retrieved from http://www.itu.int/osg/spu/cybersecurity/contributions/Ethiopia_Reba_paper.pdf.
[62]. Patrick, D. G. (2011). Managing Information Security Risk: Organization, Mission, and Information System View: U.S. Special Publication 800-39.
[63]. Mohammed, A., & Karen, N. (2009). Proceedings of the 7th Australian Information Security Management Conference: A Proposed Framework for Understanding Information Security Culture and Practices in the Saudi Context.
[64]. Fredrik. J. B. (2005). Discovering information Security Management. Stockholm: Department of Computer and Systems Sciences Stockholm University & Royal Institute of Technology.

APPENDIX A

Questionnaires to asses Information Systems Security culture and knowledge level of Users about Information Systems Security for Ethiopian Banks

This questionnaire is adopted from existing questionnaire Martin and Eloff, 2002 and distributed to collect data from sampled Ethiopian banks staffs to commence assessment of information systems security culture and level of knowledge of the users on information systems security area. The collected data is used for a thesis I am conducting for the partial fulfillment of Master's Degree in Computer Science at Hilcoe College.

Whatever information is provided will be treated with paramount confidentiality and strictly will be used for academic purpose only. There is no need to write your name.

Thank you for the time you spend for me for my educational exertion

Dawit Mekonnen
Mob: 0911921314

Biographical Data
1. Your job: _____
2. Length of service in the bank
   - 1 to 3 years
   - 4 to 5 years
   - 6 to 10 years
   - More than 10 years
3. Your educational background
   - Certificate
   - Diploma
   - Degree
   - Masters
   - Other

Knowledge Level Statement

Try to answer the following questions by using √ in the boxes which are listed in the table below

	Knowledge Statement	Yes	No	I Don't know
1	The bank has a written information security policy.			
2	I know where to get a copy of the information security policy.			
3	I have read the information security policy sections that are applicable to my job.			
4	I understand the information security policy.			
5	I know what information security is.			
6	I have taken adequate information security awareness training			
7	I know what my responsibilities are regarding information security.			
8	I am informed of security requirements to protect information			
9	I know what the risk is when opening emails from unknown senders, explicitly if there is an attachment.			
10	I know what the risk is when I share my password with other employees.			
11	I know what the risk is when I access files I am not authorized for.			
12	I know what the risk is when someone share his/her password with others employee.			
13	I know how to use the anti-virus software to scan for viruses.			
14	I have an up-to-date (recent version) antivirus in my computer			
15	When I leave my computer I always lock the screen.			
16	At the end of the day I ensure that there are no confidential documents left in my working area.			

Information Systems Security Culture Statement

Using a Likert scale (strongly agree, agree, unsure, disagree, strongly disagree) please specify to what extent you agree or disagree with the statements relating to Information systems security culture in Ethiopian banking industry.

SD= Strongly Disagree; D= Disagree; N= Neutral; A= Agree; SA=Strongly Agree

	Information Systems Security Culture Statement	SD (1)	D (2)	N (3)	A (4)	SA (5)
	Dimension: Leadership and Governance					
1	The protection of information is perceived as a top priority plan by senior management of the bank.					
2	Senior managements of the bank are committed to the protection of information assets.					
3	I believe the bank's information security strategy supports the achievement of its business objectives.					
4	I believe the risk management process of the bank are adequate to identify risks such as the threats of viruses, hackers that could negatively impact on the information of the bank.					
5	Management provides me with guidance to implement the regulatory requirements (such as client confidentiality retention of information) pertaining to information security that are required in my daily work.					
	Dimension: Security Management and Organization					
6	I believe it is necessary to commit time, people, and money to protect information.					
7	There are adequate information security specialists/coordinators throughout the bank to ensure the implementation of information security controls.					
8	I believe the information security team adequately assist in the implementation of information security control to protect information asset of the bank.					
	Dimension: Security Program Management					
9	I believe employees should be monitored on their compliance to information security policies and procedures such as measuring the use of e-mail, monitoring which site visited and what software is installed on the computers.					
10	Action should be taken against anyone who does not adhere to the information security policy (e.g. if they share passwords,					

	give out confidential information or visit prohibited internet sites).				
11	I should be seized accountable for my action if I do not adhere to information security policy.				
Dimension: User Security Management					
12	I believe there is a need for additional training to use information security controls in order to protect information.				
13	I received adequate training to use the applications I require for my daily duties.				
14	I am aware of the information security aspects relating to my job (e.g. when to change my password, which information I work with is confidential).				
15	I believe that management communicates relevant information security requirements (e.g. what internet usage is allowed, how to make backups, security usage of removable media such as USB) to me.				
16	I have adequate knowledge about emergency procedures if I have difficulty in operating the system.				
17	I accept responsibility towards the protection of information assets I use for my job.				
18	I think it is important to regard the work I do as part of the intellectual property of the bank.				
19	I believe that e-mail and internet access are for business purpose and not for personal use.				
20	I believe that the bank keeps private information (salary or performance appraisal information) confidential.				
21	I believe that sharing of password should be used to make access to information easier.				
22	I believe that IT/IS business unit implements information security controls (e.g. restricting access to secure areas, controlling access to computer systems, preventing viruses).				
Dimension: Technology Protection					
23	I believe that the information I work with is protected adequately.				
24	I believe that the information security controls (e.g. passwords) of the applications I use in my daily duties are adequate.				
25	The protection of information is predominantly the responsibility of the IT/IS business unit.				
26	I believe the incident management process of the bank is effective in resolving information security incidents.				
27	I believe the building I work in is safeguarded adequately to protect information assets.				

28	I believe the bank will be able to continue its operation if there is a disaster (e.g. fire explosion or flood) resulting in the loss of systems, people and/or premises.				
29	I know what to do in the event of disaster resulting in the loss of computer system, people, and/or premises.				
Dimension: Change					
30	I accept that some inconvenience (e.g. locking away confidential documents, making backups, or changing my password regularly) is necessary to secure information assets.				
31	I am prepared to change my working practice in order to ensure the protection of the information assets.				
32	Changes in our bank to secure information are accepted positively.				

General Security Statement

1. In your opinion what is the likelihood of people in the organization participating in accessing files they are not authorized for?
   _____

2. In your opinion what is the likelihood of people in the organization when they share their password with other employees?
   _____

3. Mention if there is a problem facing you when you perform your daily job regarding information systems security area?
   _____

4. Do you have any of the following is in place to protect your computer and electronic data? Please indicate all that apply.
   a. ___Antivirus software that is update regularly
   b. ___ Firewall
   c. ___Anti-spam filter
   d. ___Good password practice
   e. ___Others please indicate _____

5. How concerned are you about the safety of your information technology assets (computer, peripherals, electronic data, etc.)
   1. ___Very concerned
   2. ___Concerned
   3. ___Neutral
   4. ___Somewhat concerned
   5. .___Least concerned

Thank you for your unreserved cooperation

APPENDIX B

The interview questions asked by the author of this research are:
1. Do you have IS security framework in your bank, what kind of standard or framework did your bank follow?
2. What are the factors that constitute or reflect IS security culture in your bank?
3. What are the factors that have direct influence on IS security culture in your bank?
4. What are the main barriers to address the lack of IS security awareness's?
5. How can you improve security compliance in your bank?

APPENDIX C

Evaluation questions asked by the author of this research for evaluating the model are:
1. How is the applicability of the proposed framework in Ethiopian banking industry?
2. How is the usability of the proposed framework in Ethiopian banking industry?
3. How do see the completeness of the proposed framework?
4. Does the proposed framework addresses the most of the stakeholder's perception?
5. Does the proposed framework implemented with the minimum resource?
6. Are the samples used in this research satisfactory?

APPENDIX D

The overall results of the 16 IS security culture knowledge questions are displayed in Figure 4.4. The first column lists the questions and the second column the number of employees who responded to the question and their percentage figure who selected "No" respectively. The third column number of employees who responded to the question and their percentage figure who selected "Yes" respectively. The last column the total number of employees and total percentage figures who responded the question respectively.

The knowledge questions were analysed separately from the culture questions, as these two sets of questions each had different objectives. The knowledge questions are used to provide background in analysing the culture questions and they focus what employees "know". The IS security culture questions are used to measure the level of IS security culture in the bank and focus on the opinion and perception of employees regarding the information security components defined in the Information Security Culture Framework (ISCF).

Statements	No Count	No Percent	Yes Count	Yes Percent	Total Count	Total Percent
The bank has a written information security policy	42	32.6%	87	67.4%	129	100.0%
I know where to get a copy of the information security policy.	76	58.9%	53	41.1%	129	100.0%
I have read the information security policy sections that are applicable to my job.	63	48.8%	66	51.2%	129	100.0%
I understand the information security policy.	49	38.0%	80	62.0%	129	100.0%
I know what information security is.	30	23.3%	99	76.7%	129	100.0%
I have taken adequate information security awareness training.	92	71.3%	37	28.7%	129	100.0%
I know what my responsibilities are regarding information security.	35	27.1%	94	72.9%	129	100.0%
I am informed of security requirements to protect information.	47	36.4%	82	63.6%	129	100.0%
I know what the risk is when opening emails from unknown senders, explicitly if there is an attachment.	39	30.2%	90	69.8%	129	100.0%
I know what the risk is when I share my password with other employees.	16	12.4%	113	87.6%	129	100.0%
I know what the risk is when I access files I am not authorized for.	18	14.0%	111	86.0%	129	100.0%
I know what the risk is when someone share his/her password with others employee.	12	9.3%	117	90.7%	129	100.0%
I know how to use the anti-virus software to scan for viruses.	39	30.2%	90	69.8%	129	100.0%
I have an up-to-date (recent version) antivirus in my computer.	77	59.7%	52	40.3%	129	100.0%
When I leave my computer I always lock the screen	27	20.9%	102	79.1%	129	100.0%
At the end of the day I ensure that there are no confidential documents left in my working area.	24	18.6%	105	81.4%	129	100.0%
Overall Average		33.23%		66.77%		100.00%

APPENDIX E

Summary of Respondents population on the IS security culture statement on each questions

Information Systems Security Culture Statement							
Information Systems Security Culture Statement		SD (1)	D (2)	N (3)	A (4)	SA (5)	Number of total respondents
Dimension: Leadership and Governance							
1	The protection of information is perceived as a top priority plan by senior management of the bank.	13	15	25	45	31	129
2	Senior managements of the bank are committed to the protection of information assets.	8	12	35	50	24	129
3	I believe the bank's information security strategy supports the achievement of its business objectives.	9	6	24	44	46	129
4	I believe the risk management process of the bank are adequate to identify risks such as the threats of viruses, hackers that could negatively impact on the information of the bank.	7	24	39	40	19	129
5	Management provides me with guidance to implement the regulatory requirements (such as client confidentiality retention of information) pertaining to information security that are required in my daily work.	10	19	34	46	20	129
Dimension: Security Management and Organization							
6	I believe it is necessary to commit time, people, and money to protect information.	7	2	15	47	58	129

7	There are adequate information specialists/coordinators throughout the bank to ensure the implementation of information security controls.	12	18	52	32	15	129
8	I believe the information security team adequately assist in the implementation of information security control to protect information asset of the bank.	10	24	37	40	18	129
Dimension: Security Program Management							
9	I believe employees should be monitored on their compliance to information security policies and procedures such as measuring the use of e-mail, monitoring which site visited and what software is installed on the computers.	7	13	31	44	34	129
10	Action should be taken against anyone who does not adhere to the information security policy (e.g. if they share passwords, give out confidential information or visit prohibited internet sites).	10	10	33	45	39	137
11	I should be seized accountable for my action if I do not adhere to information security policy.	3	9	33	45	39	129
Dimension: User Security Management							
12	I believe there is a need for additional training to use information security controls in order to protect information.	11	6	7	40	65	129
13	I received adequate training to use the applications I require for my daily duties.	27	27	28	32	15	129
14	I am aware of the information security aspects relating to my job (e.g. when to change my	12	3	18	65	31	129

	password, which information I work with is confidential).						
15	I believe that management communicates relevant information security requirements (e.g. what internet usage is allowed, how to make backups, security usage of removable media such as USB) to me.	10	21	46	34	18	129
16	I have adequate knowledge about emergency procedures if I have difficulty in operating the system.	16	26	35	38	14	129
17	I accept responsibility towards the protection of information assets I use for my job.	7	7	21	53	41	129
18	I think it is important to regard the work I do as part of the intellectual property of the bank.	6	5	21	64	33	129
19	I believe that e-mail and internet access are for business purpose and not for personal use.	20	21	26	39	23	129
20	I believe that the bank keeps private information (salary or performance appraisal information) confidential.	15	10	24	52	28	129
21	I believe that sharing of password should be used to make access to information easier.	43	21	22	30	13	129
22	I believe that IT/IS business unit implements information security controls (e.g. restricting access to secure areas, controlling access to computer systems, preventing viruses).	14	10	30	56	19	129

	Dimension: Technology Protection						
23	I believe that the information I work with is protected adequately.	8	19	32	48	22	129
24	I believe that the information security controls (e.g. passwords) of the applications I use in my daily duties are adequate.	12	13	23	60	21	129
25	The protection of information is predominantly the responsibility of the IT/IS business unit.	13	24	28	49	15	129
26	I believe the incident management process of the bank is effective in resolving information security incidents.	7	22	47	43	10	129
27	I believe the building I work in is safeguarded adequately to protect information assets.	14	11	42	46	16	129
28	I believe the bank will be able to continue its operation if there is a disaster (e.g. fire explosion or flood) resulting in the loss of systems, people and/or premises.	16	19	39	39	16	129
29	I know what to do in the event of disaster resulting in the loss of computer system, people, and/or premises.	15	19	40	47	8	129
	Dimension: Change						
30	I accept that some inconvenience (e.g. locking away confidential documents, making backups, or changing my password regularly) is necessary to secure information assets.	12	5	20	51	41	129
31	I am prepared to change my working practice in order to ensure the protection of the information assets.	8	7	34	48	32	129
32	Changes in our bank to secure information are accepted positively.	9	11	25	52	32	129

DECLARATION

I hereby declare that the paper titled "Information Systems Security Model Using Soft Systems Methodology: Case of Ethiopian Banks" is my own work and any additional sources of information have been duly acknowledged. I confirm that neither the paper submitted nor any part of it has been published nor is being considered for publication elsewhere in any language or any form. Any contribution made to the research by others is explicitly acknowledged in the paper. I give all rights to the publishers of HilCoE Journal of Computer Science and Technology (HJCST) for provided content.

Correspondent Author's Name: _____

Signature: _____

More Books!

I want morebooks!

Buy your books fast and straightforward online - at one of the world's fastest growing online book stores! Environmentally sound due to Print-on-Demand technologies.

Buy your books online at
www.get-morebooks.com

Kaufen Sie Ihre Bücher schnell und unkompliziert online – auf einer der am schnellsten wachsenden Buchhandelsplattformen weltweit!
Dank Print-On-Demand umwelt- und ressourcenschonend produziert.

Bücher schneller online kaufen
www.morebooks.de

SIA OmniScriptum Publishing
Brivibas gatve 1 97
LV-103 9 Riga, Latvia
Telefax: +371 68620455

info@omniscriptum.com
www.omniscriptum.com

Druck:
Canon Deutschland Business Services GmbH
im Auftrag der KNV-Gruppe
Ferdinand-Jühlke-Str. 7
99095 Erfurt